LACE IN MINIATURE

LACE IN MINIATURE

ANN COLLIER

B.T. Batsford Ltd • London

Reprinted 1996

Typeset by Goodfellow & Egan Ltd. Cambridge
and printed in Hong Kong through World Print Ltd.

Published by
B.T. Batsford Ltd
4 Fitzhardinge Street
London W1H 0AH

A catalogue record for this book is available from the British Library

ISBN 0 7134 7550 1

p. 2: *Evening dress with large gigot sleeves, 1840 Showing fan (fig. 5.5), plastron (fig. 4.2) and edging (fig. 1.1)*

Title page: *Lacemaker wearing lace bonnet from p. 38*

CONTENTS

INTRODUCTION   6

1 EDGINGS AND INSERTIONS   9

2 HEAD-DRESSES   37

3 SLEEVES   45

4 COLLARS   52

5 FANS   69

6 PARASOLS   80

7 VEILS AND SHAWLS   91

8 DRESSING DOLLS   97

9 THE PATTERNS   105

FURTHER READING   123

SOURCES OF INFORMATION   124

EQUIPMENT SUPPLIERS   124

INDEX   128

INTRODUCTION

I once had a sweet little doll, dears,
The prettiest doll in the world;
Her cheeks were so red and so white, dears,
And her hair was so charmingly curled.

Charles Kingsley

Generations of children have played with dolls, but adults have used dolls, too – as funerary images, in witchcraft and as fashion models. As long ago as the Middle Ages, dolls were sent from France to the European courts as ambassadors of fashion. Possibly the first mention of such a doll is in a 1371 inventory from the French court, recording a doll and its wardrobe sent to Queen Isabella of England by her mother Queen Isabeau of Bavaria, wife of Charles VI of France. Henry IV of France also sent dolls to his bride Marie de Medici, showing her the latest French fashions. We do not know the size of these dolls but they seemed to have varied from around 18 in. to almost life-size. Anything smaller made it difficult to represent the clothes accurately.

In the eighteenth century, fashion dolls were known as Big Pandoras or Small Pandoras, depending on their size. Britain was a particularly receptive market for French fashion, which was influential throughout Europe, and even when the two countries were at war the dolls were allowed through as 'an act of gallantry to the ladies'.

After the French Revolution, however, the dolls were produced in England and were often exported to America, where they were shown to clients by dressmakers. The bodies of these dolls were usually made of wood with arms of kid leather. The visible parts were painted, and knees and elbows were jointed. Glassmakers provided coloured eyes, and wigs were made of natural hair. Wax was used for the heads and hands, and in the mid-nineteenth century a realistic skin finish was perfected in Italy by the Montanari doll-makers. Some of their work appeared in the Great Exhibition of 1851, where dolls of all ages were displayed, with eyelashes, eyebrows and hair set in wax. They were arranged as family groups in suitable settings. Wax dolls lasted only until the turn of the century, when fine porcelain heads took their place. German manufacturers became famous for their life-like dolls with bisque heads and striking expressive eyes. The Jumeau family were the best known of these doll-makers.

Portrait dolls were very popular in the nineteenth century depicting such figures as Queen Victoria, resplendent in her coronation robes, Lillie Langtry and Jenny Lind. The Queen herself had a large collection of dolls, many of which she had dressed personally. She began collecting as a young princess and continued throughout her life.

Early Regency dress (1805). Edgings from fig. 1.18 (the bottom of the dress) and fig. 1.5 (the bodice). Bonnet from fig. 2.5 and sleeve from fig. 3.5. Doll carries a fan from fig. 5.4; her dress is from fig. 8.6

In our own day, Sindy and Barbie are perhaps the nearest equivalent of the fashion dolls of earlier times. Many people collect antique and modern dolls in period costume, which is often decorated with lace. However, few lace patterns can be found small enough for dolls. Reducing the ground size, particularly in Bucks Point, makes them difficult to work – the pins are not fine enough and exceptional eyesight and dexterity are required. Cutting up antique lace to use for dolls' clothes destroys our lace heritage and should therefore be discouraged. Modern machine lace is not usually sought by the serious collector.

The size of the pattern is of the utmost importance when making lace for dolls, and in this book I have incorporated small flowers, blossoms and leaves into the designs. These can all be worked on a normal-sized pricking, in a very fine thread. I have also taken into account the time required to make the lace, especially when lengths of edging are needed, and the degree of difficulty involved. The patterns are graded thus: easy(●), intermediate (●●), complex (●●●) and very complex (●●●●).

This book contains instructions for edging, insertions, collars, fans, parasols, sleeves, bonnet backs, mittens, etc., suitable for a range of period costume, and worked using a variety of lace techniques. The bobbin lace will require some previous experience, but the needlelace can be made by beginners.

1
EDGINGS AND INSERTIONS

Lace edgings and insertions were used extensively in period dress, simple ones for underwear and elaborate flounces for outer garments. They were made in white, ecru, black or metallic thread from about the fifteenth century onwards, techniques and styles changing with fashion.

BOBBIN LACE

SIMPLE EDGINGS

- Use silk thread when a soft draping lace is required, and cotton thread for a crisp finish. A thread that is very fine in relation to the size of pricking will give a more delicate appearance to the lace.
- The antique look is best achieved by using off-white or ecru thread.
- Always use half stitch when working in black.
- Bucks Point ground gives a soft appearance and drapes well.
- Most Torchon patterns can be worked on a fine pricking using 140 thread.
- All the following edgings are suitable for long lengths, e.g. on petticoats and dresses.

BUCKS POINT

Point ground half stitch, 2 twists, pin.
Honeycomb half stitch, twist, pin, half stitch, twist.

The footside is worked with one pair of passives and a catch pin pair. For picots, twist the picot pair six times before pinning and twice afterwards. Use larger pins for the picots, as this makes them more pronounced.

With scalloped and pointed edges, passive pairs will accumulate on the headside. When taking the picot pair through these, do not weave through more than three pairs but bunch the pairs together and pass them through the picot pair. This gives a neater and firmer edge.

Always make tallies and petals the same size by counting the number of weaves.

When manoeuvring gimp thread, make one twist, pass the gimp through and make one twist after this. Tie gimps off by passing them through the bottom pair. Tie this pair once and cut off the gimps.

For fine thread and prickings, use the small, fine pins suitable for Duchesse lace.

● SIMPLE SHELL

8 pairs, 50 DMC Broder Machine (larger pattern); 120 Brok (smaller pattern)

This is the simplest and quickest of all the edgings and is suitable for long lengths. Cloth stitch and twist is used throughout, with two twists on the outer edge. This edging is shown in the photograph on p. 2.

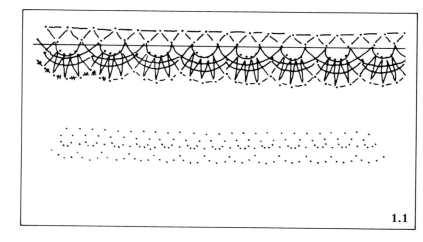

1.1

● DOUBLE PEA

11 pairs 100 Brok and 1 single gimp 30 DMC Broder Machine

A single gimp thread outlines the honeycomb rings. The edging can be worked in Torchon with cloth and twist throughout, or in point ground with honeycomb stitch for the rings and a picot edge.

1.2

● DOUBLE PEA WITH CLOTH DIAMOND

20 pairs 100 Brok and 1 single gimp 30 DMC Broder Machine

This edging is worked as for the previous one, but with the addition of a cloth or half stitch diamond. The footside has three passive pairs to give a firm edge.

1.3

● SINGLE PEA WITH LEAVES

12 pairs 100 Brok and a single gimp 30 DMC Broder Machine

A different arrangement of the gimp thread. Honeycomb stitch is used in the rings and within the gimp, with point ground everywhere else.

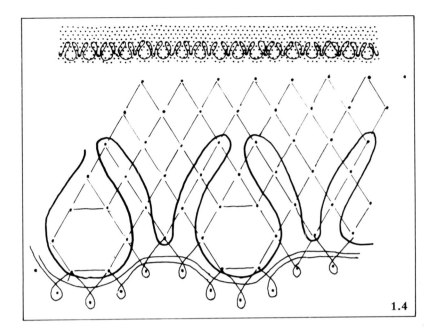

1.4

Baby doll in dress with insets, bonnet (fig. 2.1) and edgings (figs. 1.2 and 1.3). The mother doll wears a pelerine collar (fig. 4.7)

● PEA WITH STEM AND LEAVES

11 pairs 100 Brok and 1 pair gimp 30 DMC Broder Machine

The 'fingers' technique is used here to create the illusion of a small flower bud and leaves. Work in Bucks Point with point ground, using honeycomb stitch in the rings. The leaves and stem are outlined by the gimp. Picot the edge.

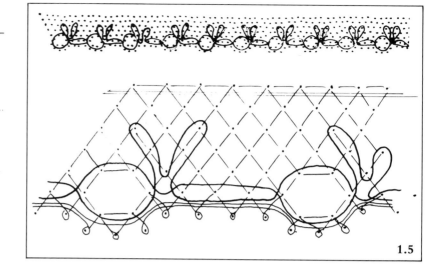

1.5

● DOUBLE PEA WITH LEAVES

11 pairs 100 Brok and 1 pair gimp 30 DMC Broder Machine

Use the same technique as in the previous edging but keep the gimp together in the scalloped edge.

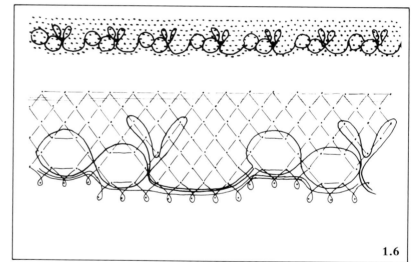

1.6

● SINGLE PEA WITH LEAF AND SHELL EDGING

14 pairs 50 DMC Broder Machine and 1 pair gimp DMC 12 perlé

The pea and leaf are worked as before but with the addition of a shell edge. This is a suitable edging for outerwear, especially in black, and is reasonably quick to work.

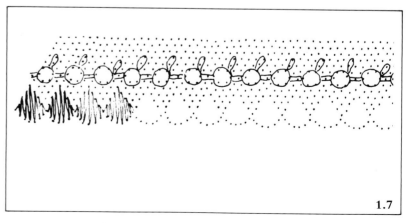

1.7

SIMPLE INSERTIONS

All the following insertions are suitable for dolls' dresses, chemises and pantaloons and are worked in 120 Brok and gimp 30 DMC Broder Machine. There is a footside on either side. Use point ground with honeycomb stitch in the rings.

● **FLOWER INSERTION**

18 pairs and 1 pair gimp

Work in point ground with honeycomb stitch within the open rings. The flowers are worked as in the diagrams and can be honeycomb rings with a cloth stitch centre, cloth stitch rings with a honeycomb ring centre, or honeycomb rings with tallies. Carry the gimp on from flower to flower.

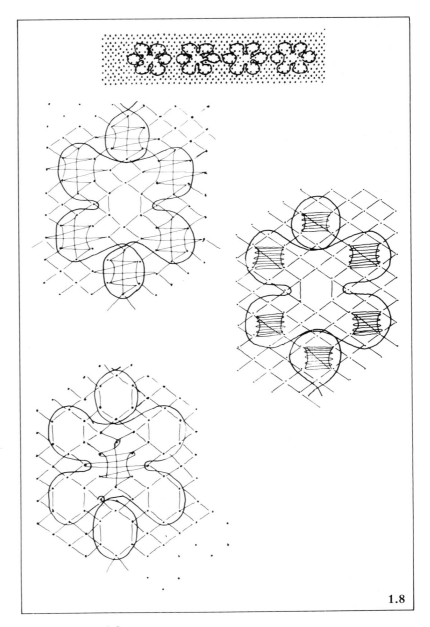

1.8

Simple edgings, from top to bottom: fig. 1.2, fig. 1.5, fig. 1.6, fig. 1.6 (enlarged), fig. 1.4, fig. 1.3

Close-up of insets from figs. 1.8, 1.9, 1.10 and 1.11

Close up of edging (fig. 1.7)

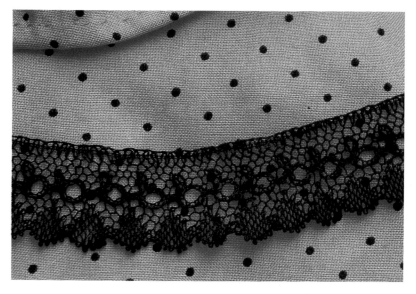

Opposite: Dress with bustle (1870), showing parasol from fig. 6.1, collar from fig. 4.4 and edging from fig. 1.7. See figs. 8.9 for bodice and sleeve

● HONEYCOMB RINGS AND TALLIES (3)

14 pairs and 1 pair gimp.

Follow diagram.

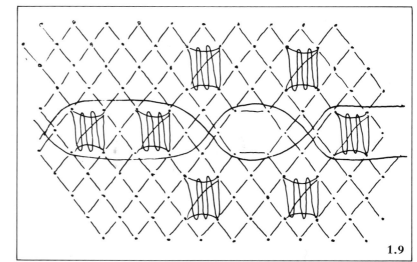

1.9

● HONEYCOMB RINGS AND TALLIES (1)

18 pairs and 1 pair gimp

Follow diagram.

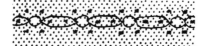

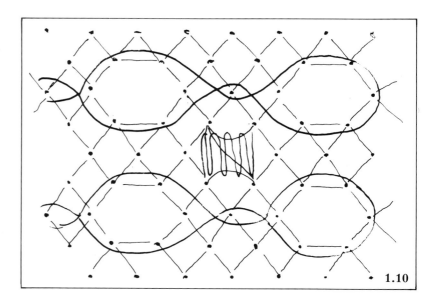

1.10

● HONEYCOMB RINGS AND TALLIES (2)

16 pairs and 1 pair gimp

Follow diagram.

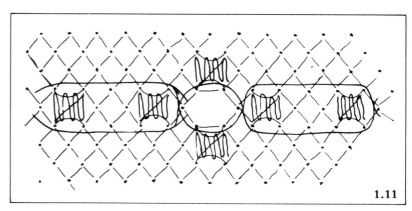

1.11

FURTHER EDGINGS

The following edgings are more complicated and take longer to work, so are suitable for short lengths such as sleeve ruffles (10 cm.) or pantaloon edges (15 cm.). They are interesting to work and pretty when finished.

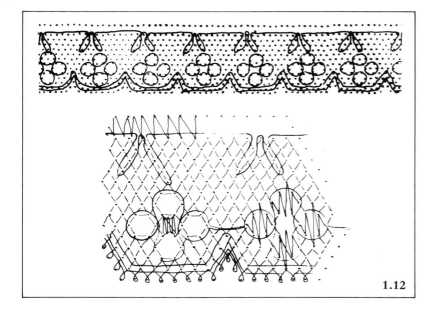

1.12

●● FOUR-PETALLED FLOWER

18 pairs 120 Brok, 3 pairs gimp, 30 DMC Broder Machine

This flower is very similar to the flower insertion on p. 13 and can be worked with cloth stitch petals and an open centre, or with honeycomb rings and a tally centre. The leaf and stalk are worked in conjunction with the footside. Honeycomb stitch is used within the gimp leaves and in between the gimps on the headside.

●● GIMP DAISY AND LEAVES

19 pairs 120 Brok, 2 pairs gimp and 1 single gimp 12 DMC perlé

Honeycomb stitch is used in the gimp fingers and in the centre ring. The gimp is passed through the ground pairs to form the daisy. Two pairs of gimp are used; one carries on from flower to flower and the other is started and cut off each time. Pairs accumulate in the headside scallop – carry these along until needed.

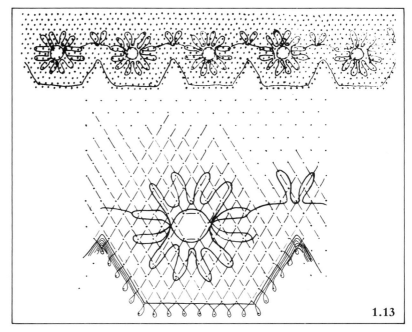

1.13

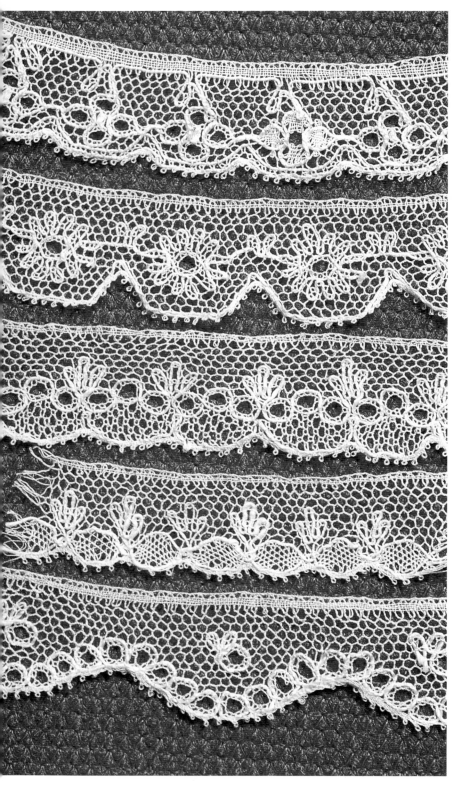

Close-up of pantaloons worn under the early Regency dress

More complicated edgings from top to bottom: fig. 1.12, fig. 1.13, fig. 1.14, fig. 1.15 and fig. 1.16

●● HONEYCOMB RINGS WITH THREE LEAVES

18 pairs 120 Brok, 1 pair gimps and 1 single gimp 12 DMC perlé

The area above the rings is worked in point ground and the area below the rings in honeycomb stitch. Use honeycomb for the rings and within the gimp leaves.

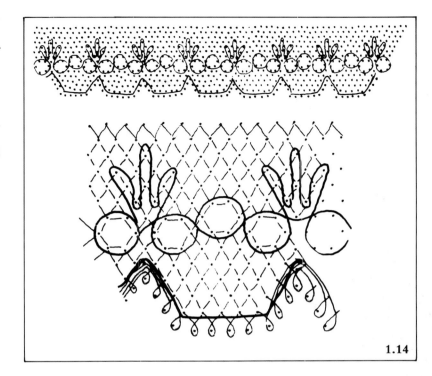

1.14

●● HALF STITCH RING AND LEAVES

16 pairs 120 Brok and 1 pair gimp 30 DMC Broder Machine

Work point ground with honeycomb stitch in the gimp leaves.

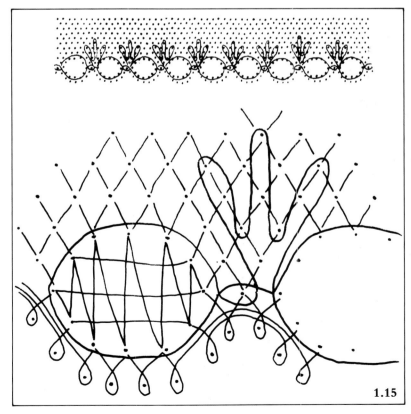

1.15

●● HONEYCOMB RING SCALLOP

20 pairs 120 Brok, 2 pairs gimp 30 DMC Broder Machine

Passive pairs accumulate on the headside. Hang in seven pairs at **A**; these will be needed later for the picots. Weave the second or third pair out for each picot and bring back in for use in the rings. Work the single pea and the leaves with a new gimp each time.

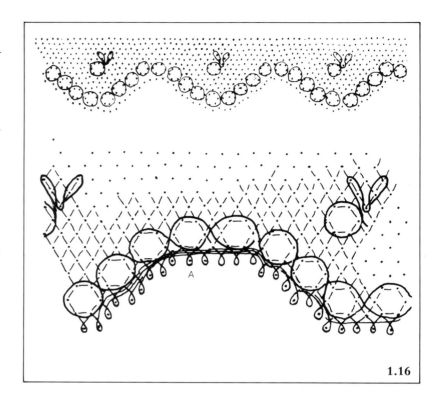

1.16

●● ROSE-BUD AND LEAF

13 pairs 120 Brok, 1 pair gimp, 1 single gimp 30 DMC Broder Machine

One gimp outlines the scallops; the other works the bud and leaf and is carried along in the foot. Use point ground with honeycomb stitch for the bud and leaf.

1.17

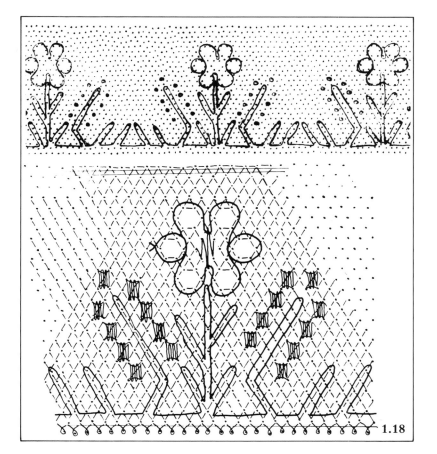

1.18

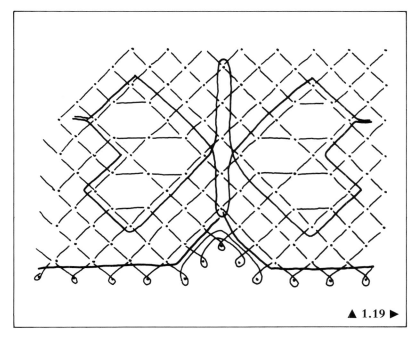

▲ 1.19 ▶

●● LARGE FLOWER WITH FERNS

30 pairs 120 Brok, 2 pairs gimp 30 DMC Broder Machine

One pair of gimps makes the leaves and stalks and the other outlines the large flower. The ferns are made with tallies on either side of the gimp stalk.

●● TORCHON BUTTERFLY EDGING

27 pairs 120 Brok, 1 pair gimp, 1 single gimp 12 DMC perlé

Follow the diagram to work the butterflies. Picots are worked using the Bucks Point technique to give a more delicate edge. The wings are in honeycomb stitch and tallies can be added if desired.

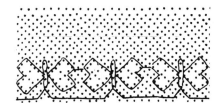

*Edgings, from top to bottom: fig. 1.17
(see also the pelerine collar in the
photograph on p. 39), fig. 1.19 and
fig. 1.18 (used at the bottom of the
early Regency dress on title page)*

*Close-up of edgings on the inner skirt
of the Georgian dress (p. 23)*

*Opposite: Georgian dress, 1740,
with edgings from figs. 1.20 and
1.21, bodice edging from fig. 1.6,
lappets from fig. 2.6, and two ruffles
from fig. 3.7*

●● TORCHON EDGE WITH SCALLOPS

29 pairs 120 Brok

The blocks can be worked in cloth or half stitch, or as spiders, alternating with blocks of rose ground.

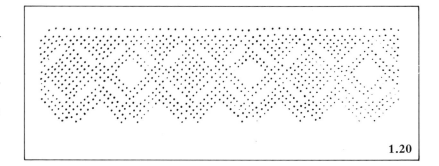

1.20

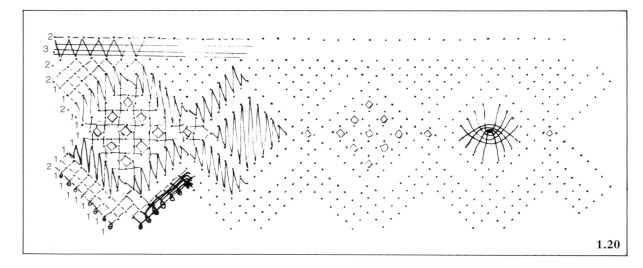

1.20

The use of the scalloped edge is unusual in Torchon lace. It is worked as in fig. 1.20. Pairs collect in the headside, so the inside pair is worked through the others and is closed with the outer pair and left to hang. Each inside pair is worked through in turn as far as **A**. The outer pair is then worked with the next one and woven through for use in **B**. Continue down the row as far as **C**.

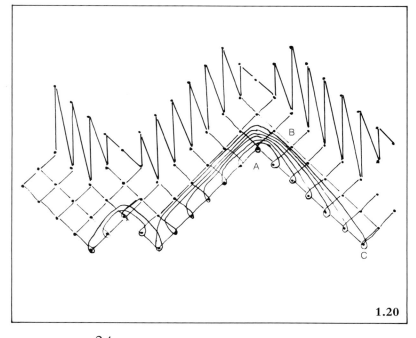

1.20

● BEDFORDSHIRE TORCHON

14 pairs 50 DMC Broder Machine

This edging is very quick to make. It has been used as a bridal coronet, and also makes a very decorative braid with picots worked on either side. It appears as part of the Georgian dress in the photographs on pp. 22 and 23.

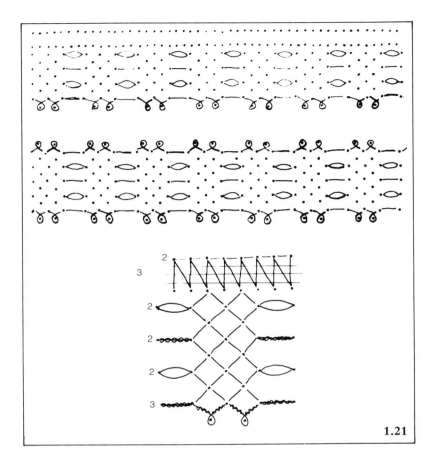

1.21

● BEDFORDSHIRE EDGING

18 pairs 50 DMC Broder Machine

This edging has a footside in cloth and twist, with a picot braid passing in and out. The headside has a nine pin edge to a narrow trail. One pair of passives travels up from the foot, through the petals and into the outer trail, returning immediately back through the petals to the foot. A sewing is made each time at **A**.

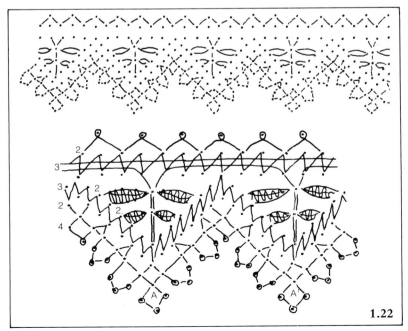

1.22

•• BEDFORDSHIRE SCALLOPS

18 pairs 120 Brok

The ground consists of plaits, while the inner ring is a plait that splits to left and right with four twists between pin holes. There are six plaited pairs, all of them in the foot from **A** to **B**. These must not be twisted. The centres can be worked in two different ways, as shown. The working will take longer if more petals are made.

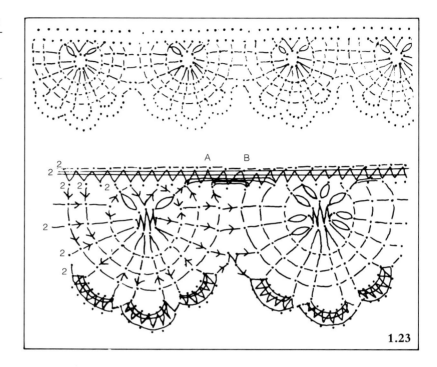

1.23

Bedfordshire edgings, from top to bottom: fig. 1.23, fig. 1.21, fig. 1.22. Collar from fig. 4.5

Opposite: *Crinoline, 1850: jacket from fig. 8.9, collar from fig. 4.5, lappets from fig. 2.8, undersleeves from fig. 3.1, and edgings from fig. 1.22. Doll carries a fan from fig. 5.9*

NEEDLELACE

The simplest forms of needlelace can be worked directly onto the edging and used to decorate necklines, sleeves, undergarments, etc. The basic stitch in needlelace is known as buttonhole. However, this is not the same as the buttonhole stitch used in embroidery, and resembles blanket or loop stitch.

BASIC STEPS

1 Trace the design on to firm tracing paper.
2 Cover with plastic film.
3 Tack firmly to a double piece of fabric (sheeting).

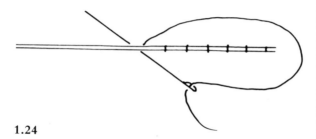

1.24

4 Couch a double thread with a finer thread (one that will break easily) round the design, through the paper and the double fabric. It will sometimes be necessary to take a single thread up and back when working a dead end, in order not to lose the double thread. Secure the couching thread at the back with a few stitches to finish. This can be started again with a knot as the threads are removed when work is finished.
5 Work filling stitches in the open areas. These are attached to the couched thread and do not go through the fabric.
6 Work bars where indicated.
7 To finish lay two threads along the same line as the original couching and buttonhole stitch closely over them.

8 Remove tacking and pull the two pieces of fabric apart, cutting the threads if necessary. If a very fine thread has been used for the couching, these threads should pull apart easily.
9 Remove the lace from the paper and pick out all the remnants of couching thread.

WORKED BARS

Take the thread across the space three times and buttonhole stitch over it.

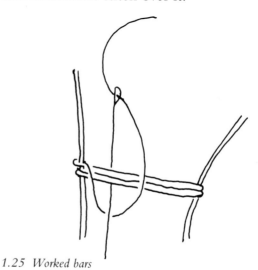

1.25 Worked bars

BRUSSELS STITCH

Introduce a thread by whipping a few stitches to the outlining. With the needle away from you, work an even row of buttonhole stitches through the couched threads so that the stitches lie on the surface. At the end of the row, take the thread under and over the couched threads and turn the work. Work the next row of stitches from left to right, with the needle towards you, into each loop of the previous row. Continue until the space is filled, then whip the filling to the upper couched threads.

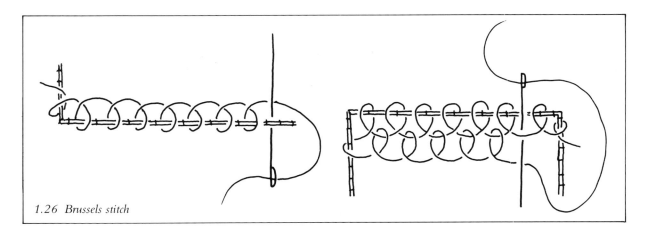

1.26 Brussels stitch

CORDED BRUSSELS STITCH

Introduce the thread by whipping a few stitches to the outlining. Work a row of Brussels stitch. When you reach the right-hand side, take the thread under and over the edge and bring it straight back to the left-hand side. Then take it under and over the outline and repeat row one, including the laid thread.

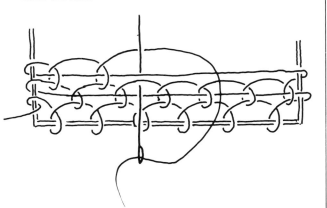

1.27 Corded Brussels stitch

DOUBLE BRUSSELS STITCH

Work a series of stitches in pairs, each followed by a two-stitch space, with the needle away from you. At the end of the row, take

the thread under the edge and turn your work so that the next row is worked in alternate pairs and two-stitch spaces, with the needle towards you.

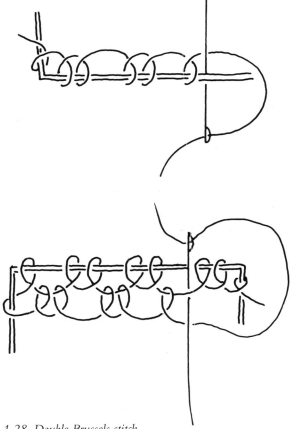

1.28 Double Brussels stitch

● LOOPED EDGING

Attach thread with a few back stitches to the edging and make a small loop to the right; attach and bring back to the left. Attach and work buttonhole stitches over these threads from left to right until the threads are covered. Attach thread and repeat for the required length.

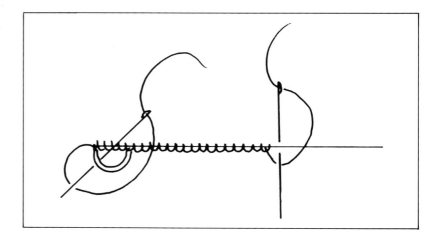

● POINT DE VENISE EDGING

Attach thread to the edging and make a buttonhole stitch into the the edge to the right. Work three buttonhole stitches into this loop and then repeat the process.

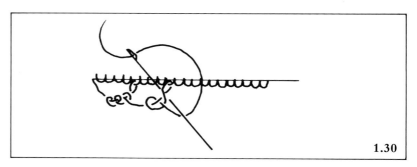

1.30

Close-up of needlelace edging from Stuart dress

Opposite: *Stuart lady, 1640. Dress pattern: fig. 8.4; needlelace edging: fig. 1.31*

● **SCALLOPED EDGING**

Brok 36

Trace the design to the required length and follow steps 1–3 on p. 00. Work the whole of the first scallop. Couch a double thread round the design along the line shown by the arrows and numbers on fig. 1.31. Start at **A** in the centre and finish at **B**. The centre will be crossed several times. The outline of area 4 has a single thread taken up and back and the couching finishes at **B**. Make small stitches, as shown, to support the final loop edge. Following fig. 1.31, work corded Brussels stitch in 1 and 3 and double Brussels stitch in 2, 4 and 5. Work bars 6, 7, 8, 9, 10, 11, 12 and 13. Work looped edge as shown in the diagram, taking the thread through the small couched stitch each time. This ensures that the loops are of an even size.

Lay two threads along the same line as the couching, and buttonhole stitch closely over them and over the couched thread. Work the next scallop and join to the first one when making the looped edge.

1.31

CARRICKMACROSS

BASIC STEPS

Remember to use cotton net with cotton organdie; silk tulle with silk organza; and nylon net with nylon organza. Use one or two strands of stranded cotton or silk with Brok 100.

1 Trace the design on to tracing paper with a fairly thick pen so that it can be seen clearly through net and organdie.

2 Cover with plastic film.

3 Place net over design and tack to paper.

4 Place organdie over the net and tack firmly to the paper. Work tack stitches in between the design to hold it firmly.

5 Oversew with fine stitches 1 mm. apart a single thread round the design in a continu-

ous flow, only stitch through the net and organdie. (The stitches must not pass through the paper, so that threads can be doubled at dead ends.) Finish off the oversewing thread with a few back stitches and start a new one in the same way.

6 When the design is complete, take out the tacking threads and remove from the paper.

7 Finish the outer edge of the design with close buttonhole stitch.

8 Carefully cut away the organdie round the design to reveal the net. (Special Carrickmacross scissors are available.) Cut back to the buttonholed edge.

The two edgings shown in the diagrams can be worked in lengths for petticoats and dresses, or worked with corners for veils, aprons, etc.

1.32 Right: ●*Shamrock edging with corner in Carrickmacross, suitable for veils and shawls*

1.33 Left: ●*Leaf edging with corner, suitable for veils and shawls*

Early Regency dress, 1815. Doll wears a pelisse and a large hat with a veil (fig. 1.33). She carries a bag made from a circle (fig. 1.6), with a border from fig. 3.3

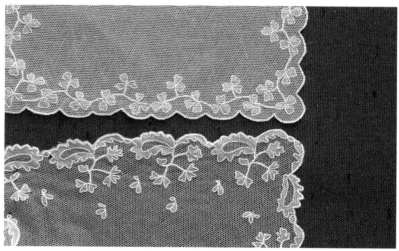

Carrickmacross edgings with corners, suitable for veils and shawls

Limerick darned edgings (fig. 1.35)

Early Regency dress, 1815. Dress pattern: fig. 8.6, with Limerick edgings (fig. 1.35). Doll carries a Bucks Point parasol (fig. 6.2)

LIMERICK

Limerick is pattern darning worked on net. Large pieces should be made in a frame but narrow edgings can be worked in the hand and are very quick to do. Use one strand of stranded cotton or silk.

FINISHING THE EDGINGS

Scallops and pointed edgings are worked by threading a coarse thread through the net and buttonhole stitching over it. A straight edge can be achieved by folding the net so that the holes align with the fold, then working zigzag darning stitches (see fig. 1.34) through the double row. Trim off the surplus net to make a firm light edging.

Various flower and leaf formations can be worked from figs. 1.35.

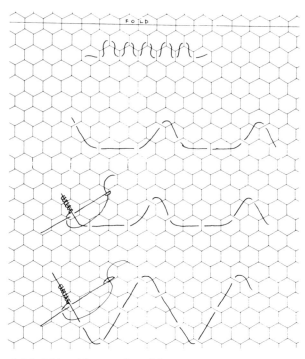

1.34 • *Limerick neatening edgings*

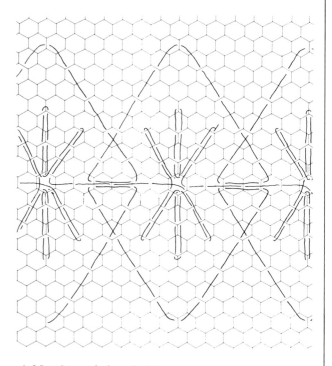

1.35 • *Limerick darned edgings*

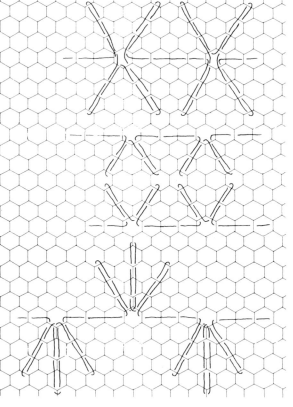

2
HEAD-DRESSES

BONNETS

Many caps and bonnets have a circular crown. The simplest style is made using a lace circle or hexagon for the back, a length of lawn or net to fit the head, and a lace frill for decoration.

Circles and hexagons can be worked in Bucks Point in sections; the angle of the ground is 60°. This method has also been used to make some of the collars, fans and parasols in later chapters and is the most satisfactory way of achieving a circular or part-circular shape.

● CIRCLE 1

17 pairs 120 Brok, 1 single gimp 30 DMC Broder Machine

Work the sections in the direction shown by the arrows and turn the pillow after each one.

It can be used with edging from fig. 1.2 for a baby's bonnet.

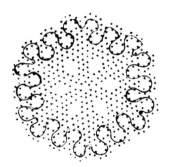

2.1

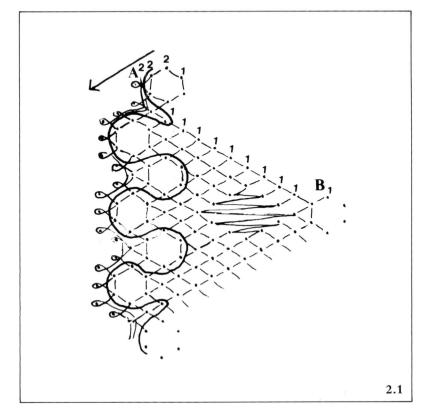

2.1

Bucks Point hexagon (fig. 2.4)

Detail of Carrickmacross bonnet (fig. 2.5)

Bonnet made from a circle (fig. 2.4). Doll also wears a lace pelerine (fig. 4.7)

Early Victorian dress, 1840. Dress pattern: fig. 8.7. Dress features gigot sleeves and pelerine collar with lace edging (fig. 1.17). See also fig. 2.5 (bonnet) and fig. 6.6 (needlelace parasol)

Three Bucks Point circles (figs 2.1, 2.2 and 2.3)

●● CIRCLE 2

**13 pairs 120 Brok, 1 pair gimp
30 DMC Broder Machine**

This has a double pea and two
leaves. Follow the arrows in fig.
2.2.

It can be used with edging from
fig. 1.6 for a baby's bonnet.

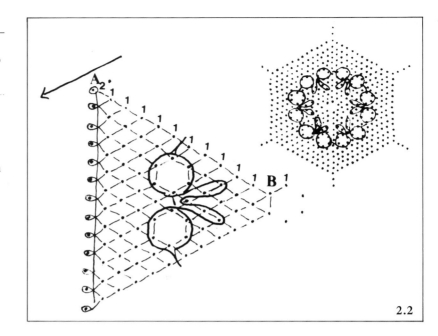

2.2

●● CIRCLE 3

**15 pairs 120 Brok or DMC 50
Broder Machine (small) 1 pair
gimp 30 DMC Broder
Machine or 12 DMC perlé
(large)**

This pattern is given in two sizes.
Follow the direction of the arrows
in fig. 2.3.

These circles are useful when
making bonnets for small dolls, and
also as bases for Dorothy bags.
They can also be used in pendants
and brooches or for cushions in a
doll's house.

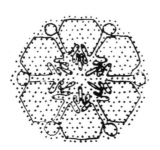

2.3

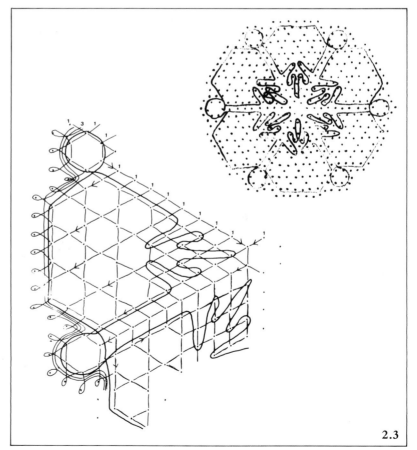

2.3

●●● HEXAGON

Suitable for a bonnet for a larger doll.

28 pairs 60 Brok, 3 pairs gimp DMC 12 perlé

Use the Bucks Point technique (see p. 37) and follow the diagram section by section. Work point ground in the star centre and honeycomb fillings in between the flowers.

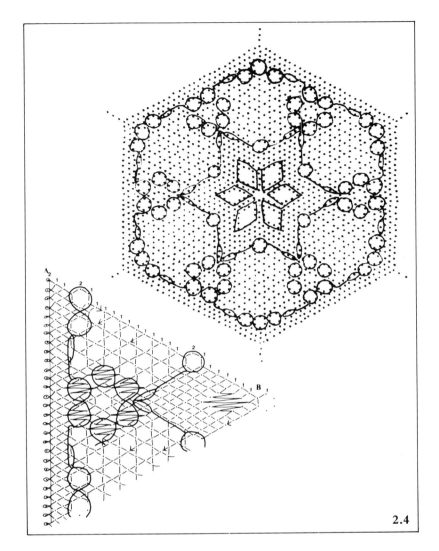

2.4

● CARRICKMACROSS BONNET

(enlarge pattern by 100%)
Work Carrickmacross as described in Chapter 1 (p. 33). Work the leaves in the centre of a circle 15 cm. (6 in.) in diameter. These is no need to finish off the edges as these are seamed in. Join **A** to **B** with a narrow seam. Gather the circle to fit. Fold a length of net 50 × 2½ cm. (20 × 1 in.) and gather to fit the lower edge. Alternatively make a 50 cm. (20 in.) length of 1 cm. (½ in.) Limerick edging.

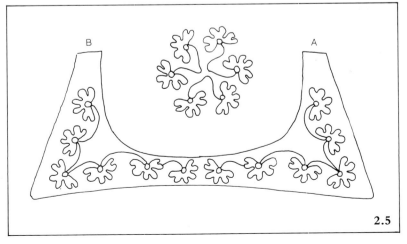

2.5

LAPPETS

Lappets were an attractive form of head decoration in fashion from the eighteenth century onwards. They continued to be worn in different forms until early in the twentieth century.

●●● BUCKS POINT CAP WITH LAPPETS (1740)

The back of the cap consists of a half-oval with a narrow frill attached to the outer edge. It is worked with 63 pairs 140 Brok, several pairs gimp 30 DMC Broder Machine

Begin at the top from **A** to **B** and work both sides simultaneously, adding and subtracting pairs as required. Work the flowers and ferns as described in Chapter 1 (fig. 1.18) and make tallies at the small circle. Add gimps where needed. Try to follow these through as much as possible. Finish the lower edge **C** to **D** by darning the threads away as neatly as possible. Make a 25 cm. (10 in.) length of edging (see fig. 1.6, p. 12) and gather this to fit the outer edge.

The lappets are made with 29 pairs 140 Brok, several pairs gimp 30 DMC Broder Machine

Start at **A** and add pairs as false picots from **A** to **B** and **A** to **C**. Tallies are marked as small circles. Work the flowers and ferns as for the back of the cap. Start new gimps on each hanging blossom and carry these along in the diagonal stalk. Take two pairs out at **D** leaving three pairs. Repeat this process to work the next diagonal to **E**, and also **E** to **F**. The ends left when the work is finished are attached to the back of the cap and darned away.

Opposite above: *Bucks Point cap and lappets (fig. 2.6). Worn in photograph on p. 23*

Late Victorian dress, 1880s, edged with Bedfordshire lace (fig. 1.23). Doll wears lappet from fig. 2.8

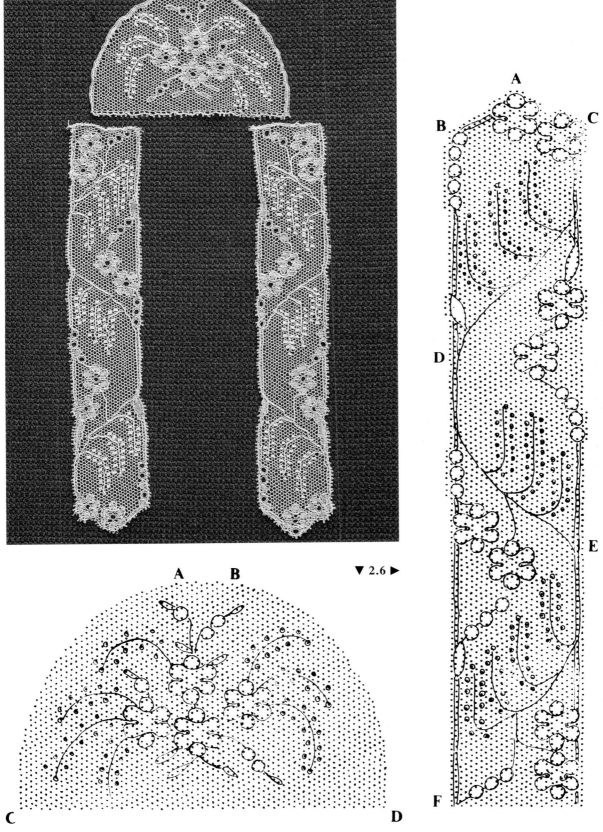

A

B

C

D

E

F

A

B

C

D

▼ 2.6 ▶

●● VICTORIAN LAPPET (left)

**42 pairs 60 Brok, 3 pairs gimp
12 DMC perlé**

Start at **A** and add pairs as required
with false picots from **A** to **B** and
A to **C**. Work flowers (as shown
in Fig. 1.8) and cloth stitch leaves,
using half stitch with the black
thread. Work tallies or clothstitch
diamonds at **X**. Reduce the
number of pairs to 14 at **D/E**, and
work a double pea edge for the
required half-length. Make a
second lappet and join to the other
half as neatly as possible.

●● BEDFORDSHIRE LAPPET
(right)

**22 pairs 60 Brok or silk of
equivalent size**

Start at **A** with four pairs and plait
to **B** on either side. Add four pairs
at **B**. Plait to **C** and add two pairs.
Work both sides simultaneously,
adding two pairs at **D** and **E**.
Work the petal from **C** and divide
at **F**. Add two pairs to make plaits
on the inside ring. Take petals in
and out of the centre, making
sewings in the centre. Take two
pairs out at **G**. Plaits must be made
with four pairs in some places, as
indicated by the thicker lines.
Work cloth and twist with four
pairs at **H**. Add four pairs at **J** and
continue as indicated, taking out
two pairs at **X**. Work half stitch
petal with 10 pairs, ending at **L**.
Bunch pairs and tie off, leaving a
tassel. Work another lappet. Lie
the tassels side by side and
buttonhole closely over them.
Cut off ends.

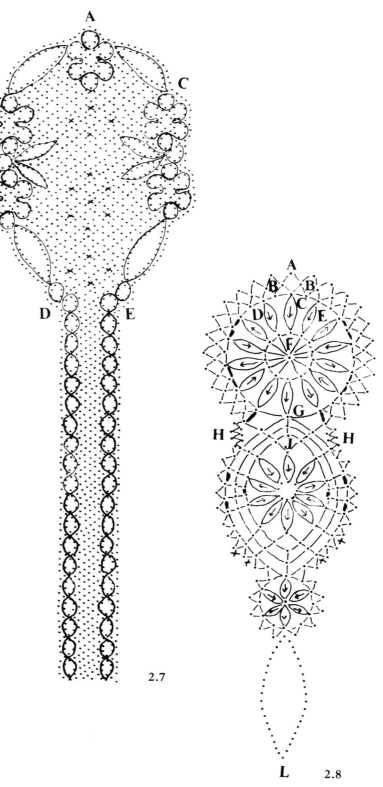

2.7

2.8

3

SLEEVES

Lace was worn on sleeves as ruffles or in borders, and sometimes complete sleeves were made of it. In the eighteenth century, sleeve ruffles were worn by both men and women, either shaped, or as straight edges gathered to fit the sleeve. The ruffles were often constructed in two or three layers, gathered to a band and attached to the sleeve; they could then be removed for laundering. Ruffles were also used in the nineteenth century, although the undersleeve trimmed with lace was more common. These were sometimes made entirely of lace, but more often they were composed of a wide lace border attached to muslin. They were then fixed loosely to the inside of the dress sleeve, or tied round the arm with tapes.

Hands were also covered by mittens, usually in lace for evening wear. Mittens could be wrist-length or reach to the elbow.

●● BORDER FOR UNDERSLEEVES

38 pairs 120 Brok, 2 pairs gimp 30 DMC Broder Machine

Bucks Point ground and honeycomb were used in this pattern.

Begin at **A** and **B**. The gimp makes 'fingers' from a cloth stitch diamond at **A**. A new gimp is started each time at the top of this diamond and doubles up with the first one for a short distance before cutting out. Short lengths of gimp are all that is necessary. Join the strip to form a ring and attach to a strip of lawn of the same size. Put a draw-string at the lace headside and at the top of the lawn, and gather to fit the arm.

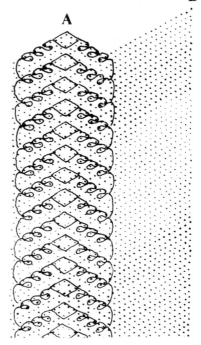

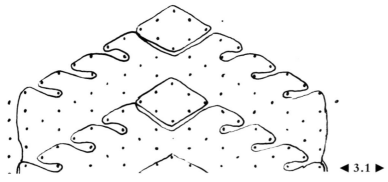

◄ 3.1 ►

Late Victorian evening dress, 1880s. Dress pattern: fig. 8.11. Doll carries a fan from fig. 5.3 and wears a coronet (fig. 1.21) and mittens (fig. 3.4)

Bucks Point lappet from fig. 2.7 and Bedfordshire lappet from fig. 2.8

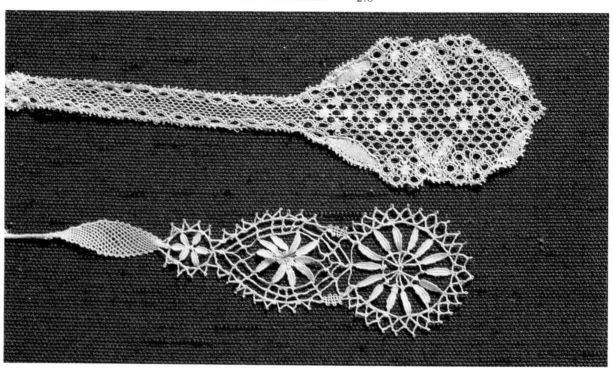

Mittens (figs. 3.2 and 3.4) with dolly bag (fig. 3.3)

● POINT GROUND BORDER FOR SLEEVE EDGES, MITTENS OR DOLLY BAG

24 Pairs 50 DMC Broder Machine, 2 pairs gimp 12 DMC perlé

This has two shell edges worked as in fig. 3.2, using the pivot pin **A** several times. Work in cloth and twist with three twists on the outer edge. The central pea and leaves design is worked as in fig. 1.5 on p. 12.

The pattern shown can be joined into a tube for mittens, with the doll's thumb pushed through the ground. Work twice or three times this length to make the top for a dolly bag; join as a tube and sew to a round base using fig. 2.2 on p. 40.

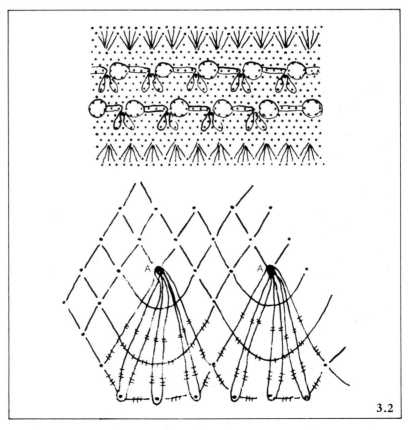

3.2

●● GIMP STAR EDGING

33 pairs 120 Brok, several gimps 30 DMC Broder Machine

This has a double shell edge as in fig. 3.2, with gimps forming the star design. Diagonal gimps pass through the star and are taken in at the top of the shell to pass out for the next diagonal. Work the star from the diagram; a new gimp is needed for each one.

This pattern can also be used for edges, mittens and dolly bags.

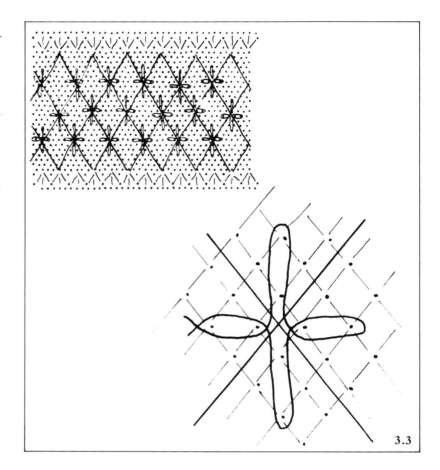

3.3

●● ELBOW MITTENS

47 pairs 50 DMC Broder Machine, 5 pairs gimp 12 DMC perlé

This pattern is worked using the Bucks technique with point ground and honeycomb stitch in the rings and the gimp leaves.

Set up two pairs on each pin from A to **B** and begin at **A**. The flowers are worked as in fig. 1.8 on p. 13 with gimp finger leaves. Gimps are added. Finish at the base and leave the threads to join. The doll's thumb is pushed through the ground.

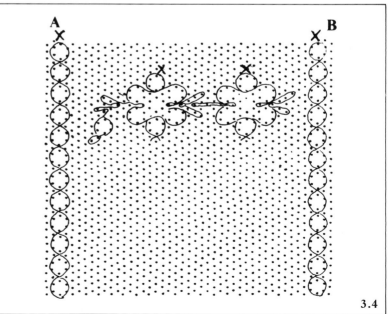

3.4

●●● COMPLETE SLEEVE USED ON THE REGENCY DRESS

38 pairs 120 Brok, 2 pairs gimp 30 DMC Broder Machine

This incorporates the edge pattern in fig. 1.14. The shaping is achieved by adding and decreasing pairs as necessary on the curved edge. This pattern needs no foot as the edge is sewn into the armhole.

Work the extra piece at **A** so that it can overlap at **B** when making up the sleeve. Tallies (marked with an x in the diagram) are used to break up the plain net.

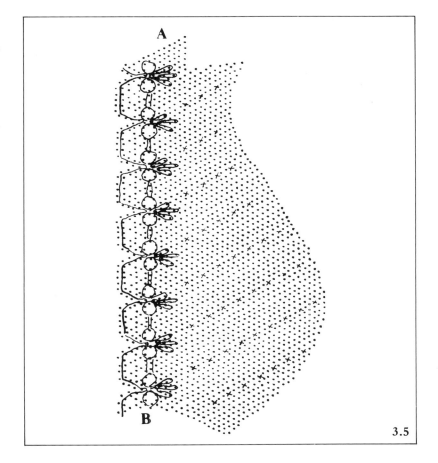

3.5

●● SINGLE BUTTERFLY RUFFLE

27 pairs 120 Brok, 2 pairs gimp 30 DMC Broder Machine

This can be worked in Torchon or point ground but with picots on the headside. Work the butterflies as in fig. 1.19 (p. 21). Add pairs as the width increases and take them out as it reduces. Pairs will accumulate in the headside in the scallops; carry these along as directed in Chapter 1; they will be needed later.

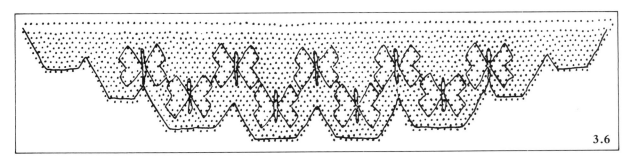

3.6

Butterfly ruffle (fig. 3.6), Regency sleeve (fig. 3.5) and undersleeve with lace border (fig. 31.)

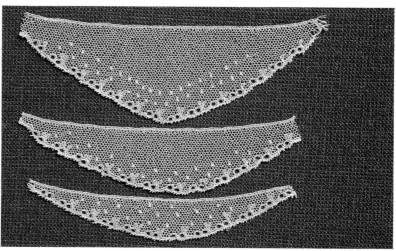

Three sleeve ruffles (fig. 3.7)

●● THREE RUFFLES

**Large ruffle: 47 pairs 60 Brok,
1 pair gimp 30 Broder
Machine
Medium ruffle: 34 pairs 60
Brok, 1 pair gimp 30 Broder
Machine
Small ruffle: 23 pairs 60 Brok,
1 pair gimp 30 Broder
Machine**

The design shown in fig. 3.7 has
three ruffles, each ending in the
pea edge. Trace off each
separately.

When making separate ruffles,
add tallies at intervals as seen in the
photograph to break the otherwise
plain net. Point ground is used
throughout with the pea design as
in fig. 1.6 on p. 12.

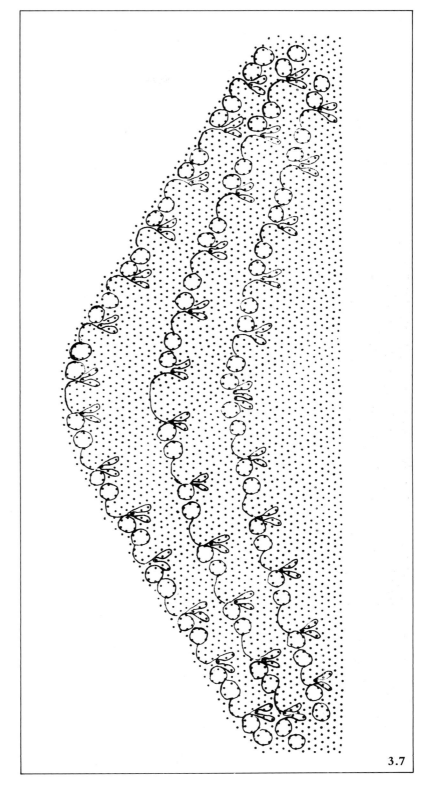

3.7

4
COLLARS

Lace has been used for decoration at the neckline for centuries. The Elizabethans wore extravagant ruffs with spiky edges of needlepoint or bobbin lace. This fashion was followed by the fall collar, which was of softer lace and usually had cuffs to match. Ruffs and fall collars were worn by both men and women. Heavy Venetian Gros Point was very popular for gentlemen's cravats.

Men gradually stopped wearing lace and little more than lace jabots and frilled cuffs lasted through the Georgian period, to disappear entirely by Victorian times. In the seventeenth and eighteenth centuries women's clothing often featured very low necklines edged with lace. In addition, lace frills were sometimes gathered round the neck. Collars were less common in the early Regency period, but by 1820 large lace cape collars called pelerines were very fashionable and Bertha collars were worn for evening. The Victorian era saw the wearing of lace collars in all forms, from small Peter Pans to very large Berthas. Antique lace was frequently used, often remodelled to suit the fashion.

The dresses of the 1890s had collars with splits to accommodate the very large gigot sleeves, often with cuffs, belts and panels to match. Heavy Venetian lace was in fashion again and small boys were dressed to resemble Little Lord Fauntleroy.

The following patterns fit different necklines and suggestions for use can be seen in the illustrations.

●● PLASTRON 1 (left)

23 pairs 60 Brok, 2 pairs gimp
12 DMC perlé

This pattern is worked using the Bucks Point technique. Start at **A** and add pairs where necessary to **B**. Work down to **C** and finish the threads off in the cloth stitch trail from **C** to **D**. Make a second piece, reverse it, and join at **AB**. Alternatively, those with experience of Bucks Point may prick out the pattern twice and join **AB**.

Begin at **C** to **D** and work down to **AB**, leaving pairs out from **A** to **B**. Turn the work and make the second half with the pairs hanging from **A** to **B**. This turn is quite difficult to achieve neatly; no extra pairs are needed but some pin holes are used twice.

●● PLASTRON 2 (right)

28 pairs 60 Brok, 3 pairs gimp
12 DMC perlé

Work using the Bucks Point technique. This is more complicated than the previous pattern, though the method is the same as for Plastron 1. The flowers are worked as in fig. 1.8 (p. 13) and the zigzag edge as in fig. 4.6 (p. 57). Picots are worked on both sides.

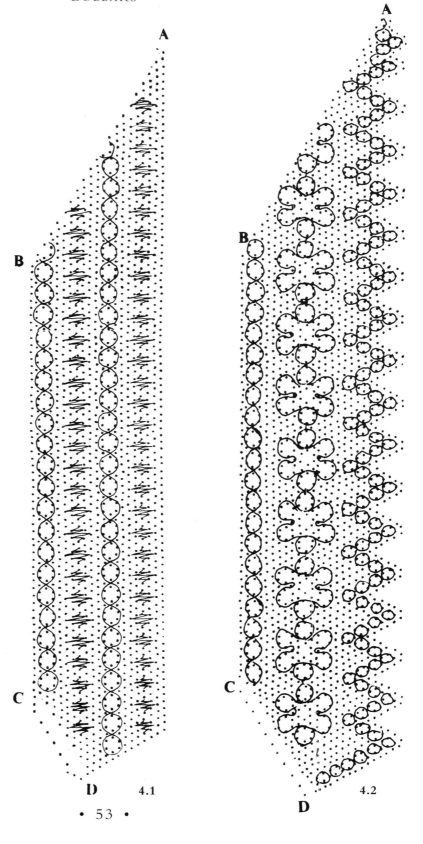

4.1

4.2

Children of the 1880s, copied from a Victorian print. Girl doll wears a Carrickmacross collar (fig. 4.9), with sleeve edgings from fig. 1.35. The boy doll wears a suit featuring a needlelace collar and cuffs from fig. 4.10

Opposite: Children, 1840. Girl doll wears a plastron from fig. 4.1

Below right: Detail of plastron from fig. 4.2, as worn on the evening dress in the photographs on p. 2

Below left: Neck ruffle from fig. 4.3, gimp border from fig. 3.3 and detail of plastron from fig. 4.1

•• THE NECK RUFFLE

14 pairs 120 Brok, 2 single gimps 30 DMC Broder Machine

Work using the Bucks Point technique. This is a double version of fig. 1.4 (p. 11) with a double footside. Run a gathering thread through the centre and draw up to fit the neck. This pattern can be used as an edging or as a garter.

•• BERTHA COLLAR

36 pairs 60 Brok, 2 pairs gimp 12 DMC perlé

Work using the Bucks Point technique. This pattern is worked as an edge, but shaped so that it is deeper at centre back.
CD is centre back, reverse the pattern for the whole collar. Start at **A** and add pairs first at the footside and headside to **B**, and then only on the footside. Reduce pairs on the footside as the collar narrows. Gather the lace slightly to fit the neckline and shoulders. Remember to work in half stitch if using black thread.

4.3

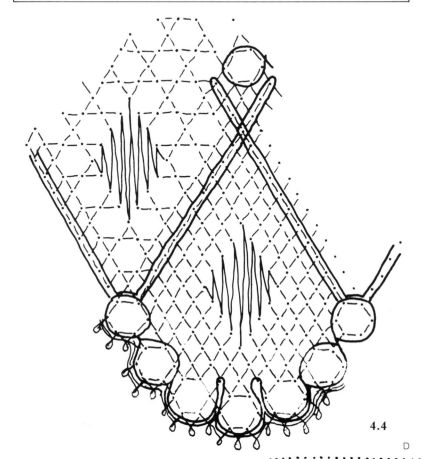

4.4

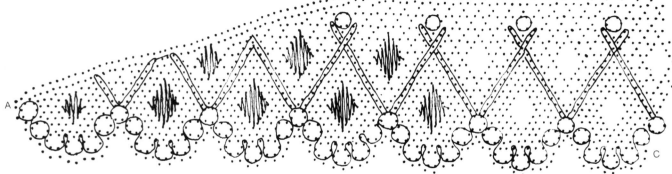

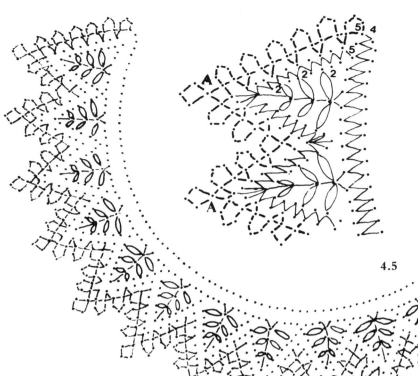

4.5

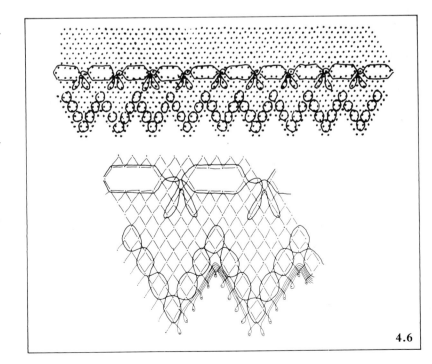

●● SMALL COLLAR

20 pairs 60 Brok

Work using the Bedfordshire technique. This pattern is worked in a similar way to the edging in fig. 1.22, but with more petals and a wider foot with 4 prs passives. Plaits and picots form the edge with a sewing at **A**.

This pattern has been used for the curved boot tops of the Cavalier on p. 58.

●●● COLLAR AND CUFFS

CUFFS

26 pairs, 140 Brok, 2 pairs gimp 30 DMC Broder Machine

This pattern features a straight Bucks edge with large honeycomb ovals, gimp leaves and an indented edge of four pin honeycomb rings. Follow the diagram for the length required; this will usually be 6 cm. (2¹/₂ in.)

4.6

Detail of Bertha collar (fig. 4.4). See photograph on p. 15

Cavalier and lady, 1640. The Cavalier doll's outfit is from fig. 8.5. He wears a collar and cuffs from fig. 4.6 and boot tops from fig. 4.5

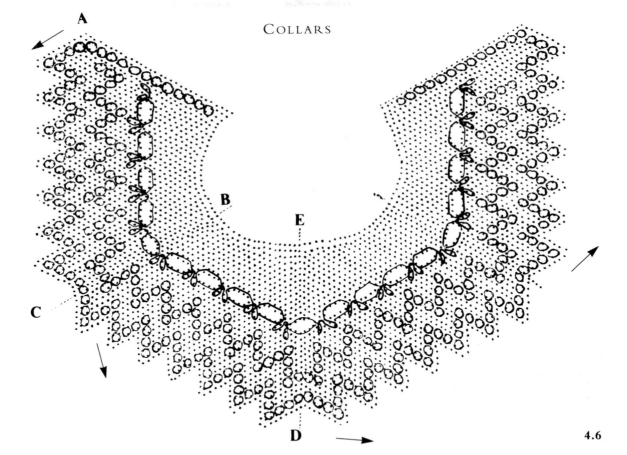

4.6

COLLAR

41 pairs 140 Brok, 4 pairs gimp 30 DMC Broder Machine

Work using the Bucks hexagon technique, making the cuffs first to familiarize yourself with the technique before attempting the collar.

This is worked as a Bucks hexagon but with only four segments instead of six. Start at **A** and work in the direction of the arrows to **BC**. Turn and work the next segment. Continue to **DE**; pairs will accumulate on the neck edge, but do not remove these as they will be needed later.

Collar and cuffs worn by the Cavalier in the photograph on p. 58 (see fig. 4.6)

●●● PELERINE COLLAR

**40 pairs 60 Brok, 2 pairs gimp
12 DMC perlé**

Work using the Bucks hexagon technique. This pattern is made in segments and is worked a segment at a time. However, because of its shape, pairs have to be added on the curves and taken out in the hollows. Start at **A** and work in the direction of the arrows to **BC**. Begin the next segment at **C** and work to **DE**. Work cloth stitch mayflowers or tallies at **X**. The inner border is point ground with peas and leaves (see fig. 1.5, p. 12).

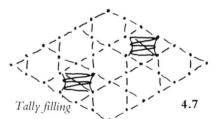

Tally filling   **4.7**

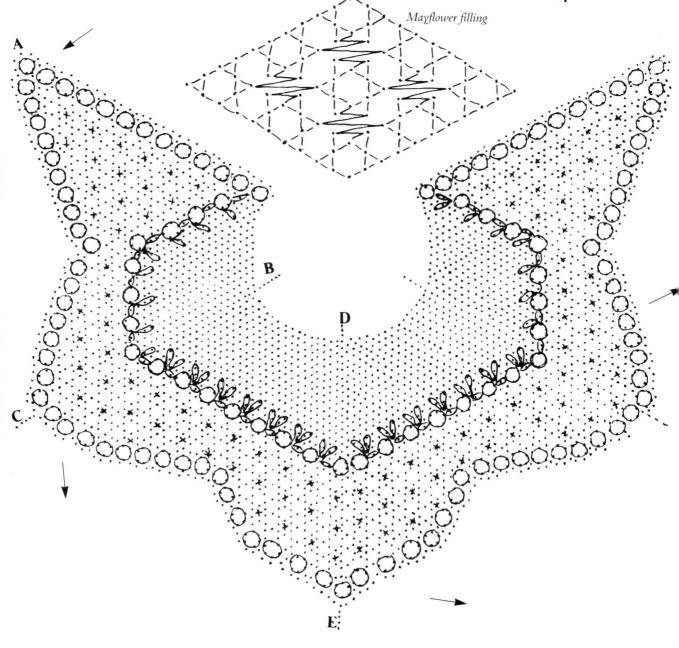

Mayflower filling

●● ROUND COLLAR AND CUFFS

32 pairs 50 DMC Broder Machine, 3 pairs gimp 8 DMC perlé

This pattern uses the Bucks technique worked on a curved pricking. Reverse pattern at **CB** for complete collar pricking. Start at **A** with false picots, introduce gimp at **B** and work from **A** to **C** and **B** to **D**. Begin trail at **E**; this accommodates the pairs that come in and out of the two sizes of ground. Use the gimps in the trail at **D**.

Work the cuffs in the same way, using the following threads: 22 pairs 50 DMC Broder Machine, 2 pairs gimp 8 DMC perlé. This pricking, if extended, will make a Peter Pan collar.

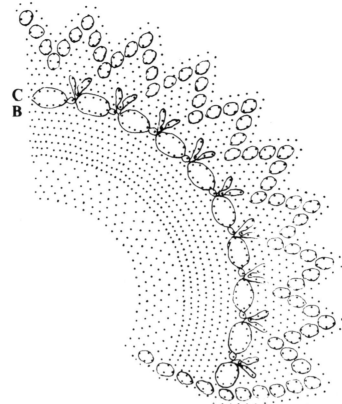

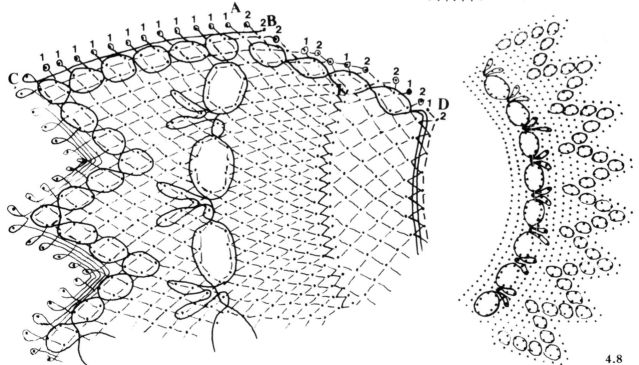

4.8

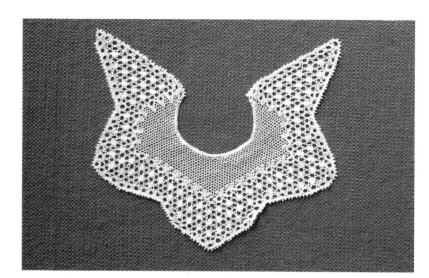

Pelerine collar (fig. 4.7)

Round collar and cuffs (fig. 4.8)

Carrickmacross collar (fig. 4.9), worn in the photograph on p. 54

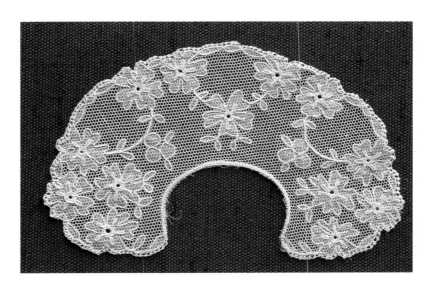

●● CARRICKMACROSS FLOWERS

Follow the general instructions for Carrickmacross on p. 33. Buttonhole stitch the edge firmly round the whole collar and work Point de Venise as in fig. 1.30 (p. 30) round the outer edge. Cut away the organdie and make French knots in the berries, buttonhole stitch rings in the flower centres, and 'lazy daisies' in the petals.

4.9

●● NEEDLELACE COLLAR AND CUFFS

Work in 30 DMC Broder Machine cotton to give the heavy look of Venetian lace. Trace off the patterns and follow the general instructions for needlelace on p. 28.

Work Brussels stitch in the outer edges.

Work corded Brussels in **1**, as well as for leaves, edges and flower centres.

Work bars and wheels where indicated.

Work Beading in **2** and in petals and fern frond.

Finish the edge with loops as in fig. 1.31.

Make a small tassel and cord to tie at neckline centre front.

4.10

NEEDLELACE TECHNIQUES

The follow techniques will be required when making the Needlelace Set on pp. 67–8.

BEADING

This is useful for filling a narrow space. Work a row of buttonhole stitches on either side of the area and join each loop with several loose oversewn stitches – the loops lie side by side.

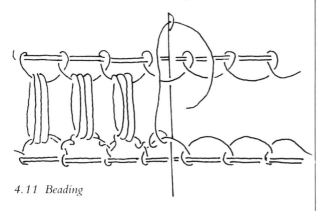

4.11 Beading

WOVEN WHEELS

These are useful for filling a circular space. Take the thread across the space from **1** to **2**; whip back over the thread to **1**. Now whip along the outline to the next strut at **3**, cross to **4** and back, whip along from **3** to **5**, **5** to **6** and back, **5** to **7** and **7** to **8**. Whip back as far as the centre and complete the wheel by darning in and out of the struts. Since there is an even number of struts, it is necessary to work over two and under one periodically. Do not work this in the same place each time. Finally anchor the thread in the centre and whip back to **7**.

BUTTONHOLE WHEELS

Take a thread from **1** to **2** (twice), back to **1** and buttonhole back to **2**. Whip to **3**, take the thread from **3** to **4** (twice), back to **4** and

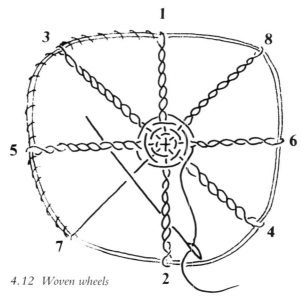

4.12 Woven wheels

buttonhole to **3**. Take a stitch through the centre. Whip to **5**, take a thread from **5** to **6** (twice), back to **6** and buttonhole to **5**.

Whip to **7**, **7** to **8** (twice), back to **8**, buttonhole to **9**. Take a thread three times round, a short distance from the centre. Buttonhole over these threads round to **9**. Continue the buttonhole from **9** to **7** and fasten off.

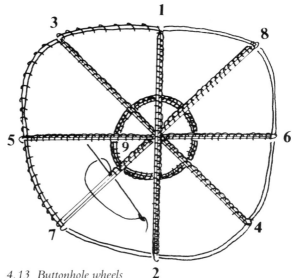

4.13 Buttonhole wheels

*Lady, 1890s. Dress pattern: fig.
8.12, decorated with needlelace from
figs 4.14 and 4.15*

*Collar and cuffs from figs 4.14 and
4.15, as worn in the photograph.*

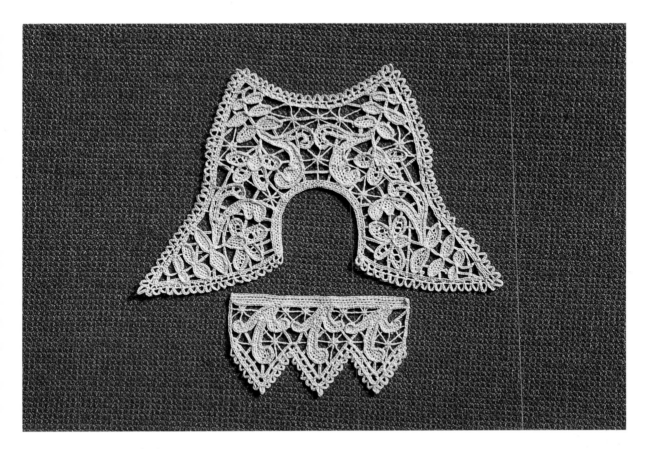

Needlelace collar and cuffs (fig. 4.10),
as worn in photograph on p. 54

NEEDLELACE SET

Work in 30 DMC Broder
Machine thread to give a heavy
effect.

● **SMALL COLLAR AND CUFFS**

Follow the general instructions on
p. 28. Outline in two rows of
Brussels stitch. Work bars where
indicated and wheels as in fig. 4.13.

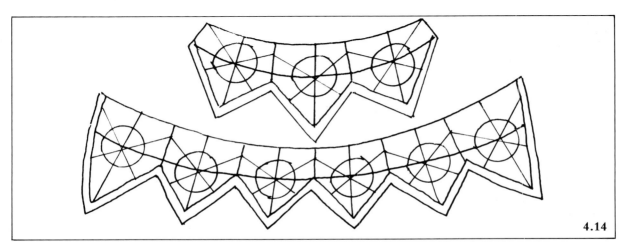

4.14

●●● LARGE COLLAR, BELT AND DRESS STRIP

Work Corded Brussels in all leaves and small flowers. Double Brussels in the large flowers and buttonhole stitched wheels as in fig. 4.15. Make bars where indicated. Buttonhole the outer edge and work Point de Venise on to this to give a picot finish.

4.15

5
FANS

Fans have been used for centuries but lace fans first became popular only in the late Georgian period. Their heyday was in the Victorian era, when a great variety of lace techniques were employed in their construction. They were carried and flirted with at all dances, and were used instead of, or as well as, a posy at weddings. The following patterns fit the small plastic fans that are available today (see Equipment Suppliers).

● **TORCHON 1**

25 pairs 50 DMC Broder Machine, 1 pair gimp 8 DMC perlé (for a heavy look) or 25 pairs 100 Brok and 12 DMC perlé (for a lighter look)

This pattern can be reduced to 70% and worked in Brok 160 for ½ scale fans and parasols.

Work on a curved pricking with rose ground and four petalled flowers. Start at **A** and work in the direction indicated, ground lines are curved. Work the shell edge as in fig. 3.2 (p. 47).

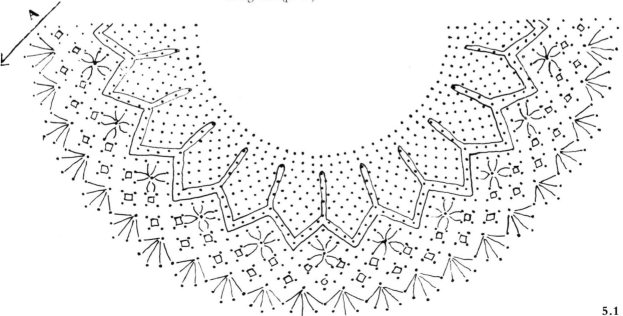

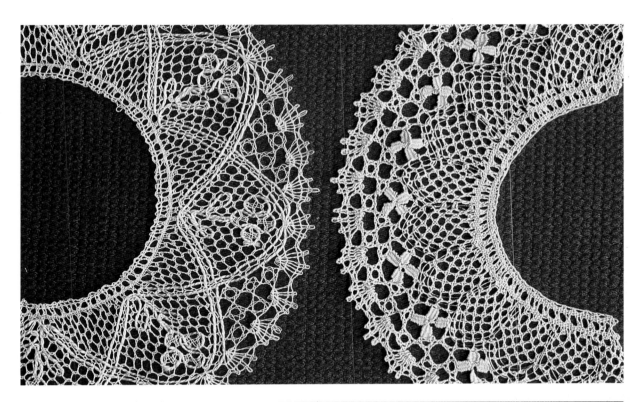

Detail of Torchon fans from figs. 5.1 and 5.2

Opposite: *Late-Victorian wedding dress, 1870s. Dress pattern: fig. 8.10. Bride carries a posy with lace from fig. 5.2, and wears a coronet (fig. 1.21) and wedding veil (fig. 7.2)*

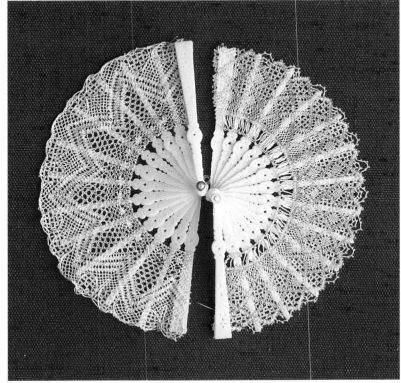

Cream and gold fan (fig. 5.3); silver and white fan (fig. 5.4)

● TORCHON 2

25 pairs, 3 pairs gimp (thread size as for Torchon 1)

This pattern can be reduced to 70% and worked in Brok 160 for ¹⁄₁₂ scale fans and parasols.

Short lengths of gimp surround the flowers. Torchon and rose ground are used with a shell edge as in fig. 3.2.

Start at **A** and work in the direction indicated; ground lines are curved. If made into a circle, Torchons 1 and 2 can be used to make a parasol or a circular collar. The fine thread version has been used on the bride's posy (see p. 70).

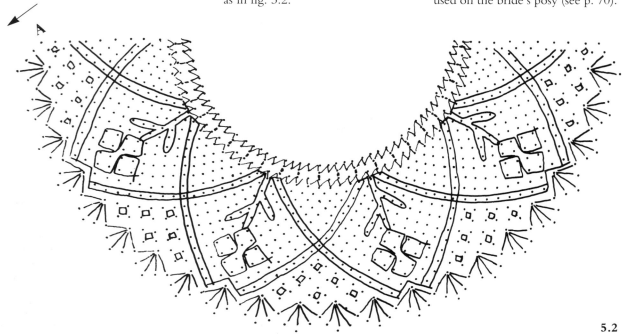

5.2

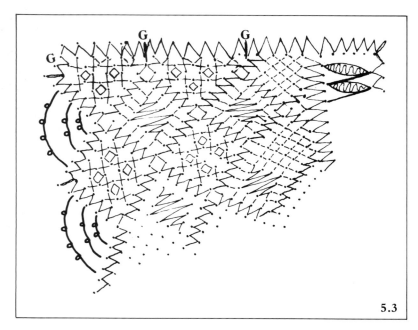

5.3

●●● CREAM AND GOLD

42 pairs ecru Brok 140, 3 pairs fine gold 'Effektgarn'

This pattern is also worked on a curved pricking but with a very fine ground. Each trail has a gold weaver introduced at **G**. Rose ground blocks alternate with half stitch blocks. Take out plaits with picots as indicated on the outer edge. Petals are used at the base in between the two trails, out as a petal and back as a plait. Follow the diagram.

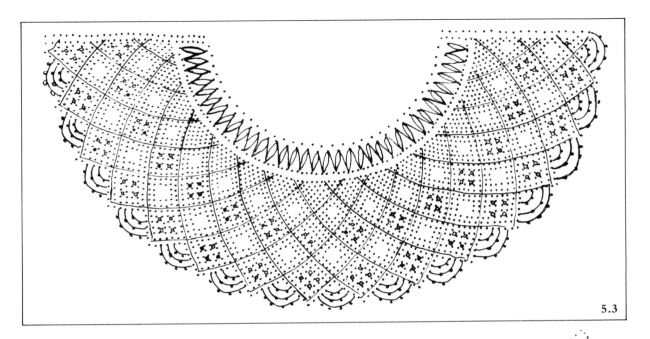

5.3

●●● SILVER AND WHITE

30 pairs 140 Brok white, 12 pairs fine silver 'Effektgarn', 1 silver gimp Twilleys Silver Dust

The silver gimp outlines the butterflies, which are in rose ground. The gimp doubles round the curve and pairs of white are twisted round it each time, to come in for the Torchon ground. Honeycomb ground is used in the lower sections. Silver threads are used in the lower section from **B** to **C**; these will stay in position if whole stitch is used instead of half stitch. One silver pair is introduced at **A** as weavers.

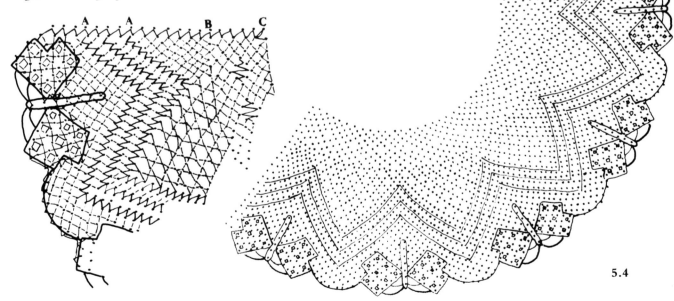

5.4

Floral Bucks fan (fig. 5.6);
Carrickmacross fan (fig. 5.7)

Bucks Point fan (fig. 5.5). See
photograph on p. 2

●●● BUCKS FAN

38 pairs 100 Brok or black 80 Madeira, 6 pairs gimp 12 DMC perlé

Three sections are worked; use the hexagon technique. Follow the diagram. Start at **A** and work in the direction indicated. Work leaves in cloth stitch if using white thread, or half stitch if using black. Picot both headside and footside. Make the next two sections in the same way.

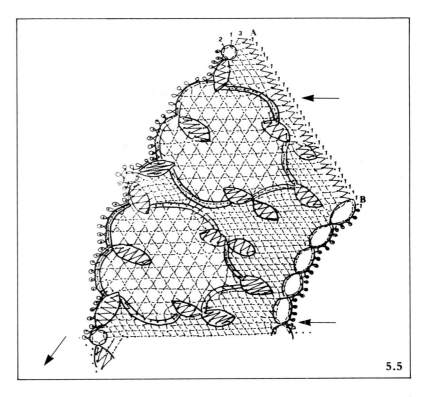

5.5

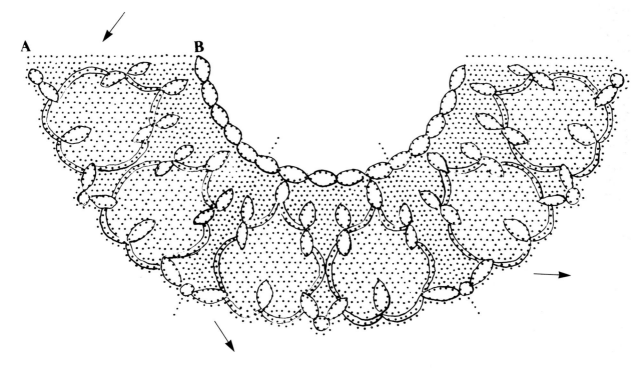

●●● FLORAL BUCKS FAN

36 pairs 140 Brok, several gimps 30 DMC Broder Machine

Work using the hexagon technique. Although there are three sections to this fan, each one is different. However, the technique, working each at a different angle, is the same. Turn the pillow where the segment line is indicated. The patterning is worked in the same way as the back of the cap in fig. 2.6 (p. 43) and the edging in fig. 1.18 (p. 21). Picots are made at both headside and footside.

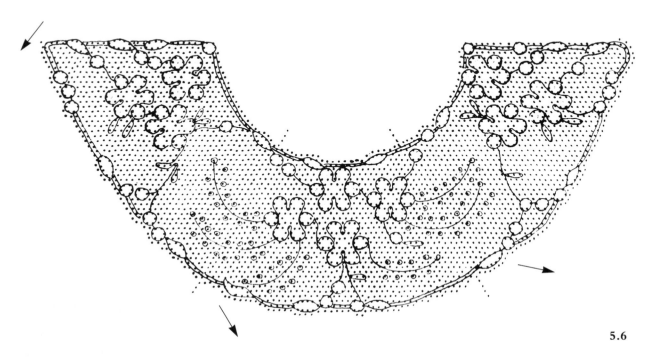

5.6

PEA STITCH

Work the first row as for Brussels stitch from left to right with the needle away from you. Turn, and with the needle towards you, work two stitches and miss two stitches. Turn and work three stitches in the large loop and one stitch in the small loop.

Repeat the second row, making sure that the two worked stitches come in the centre of the previous large loop and the missed stitches are over the small loop.

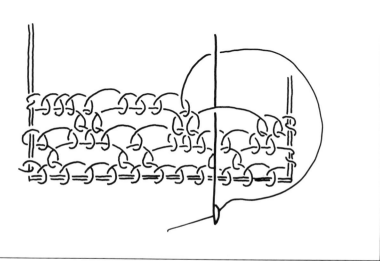

●● CARRICKMACROSS FLOWERS

Follow the general instructions for Carrickmacross (p. 33). Work Point de Venise on the outer edge and buttonhole stitch the base. Cut away to this.

Work French knots in the centres of the small flowers and buttonhole stitch rings in the large flowers.

5.7

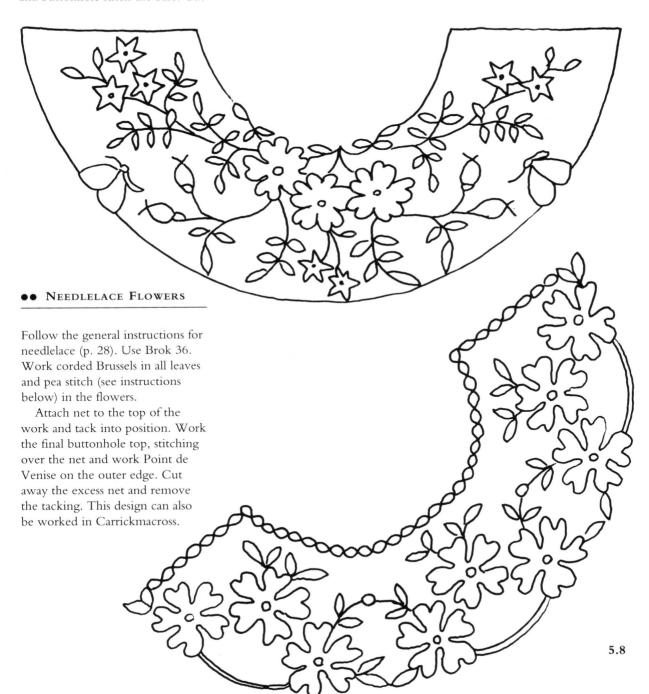

●● NEEDLELACE FLOWERS

Follow the general instructions for needlelace (p. 28). Use Brok 36. Work corded Brussels in all leaves and pea stitch (see instructions below) in the flowers.

Attach net to the top of the work and tack into position. Work the final buttonhole top, stitching over the net and work Point de Venise on the outer edge. Cut away the excess net and remove the tacking. This design can also be worked in Carrickmacross.

5.8

Needlelace flower fan (fig. 5.8); needlelace fan shown in photograph on p. 27 (fig. 5.9)

PYRAMID STITCH

Work a row of Brussels stitch.

Turn and work two miss two.

Turn and work one miss three (over the same loop).

Turn and work three in every large loop.

Turn and repeat the sequence.

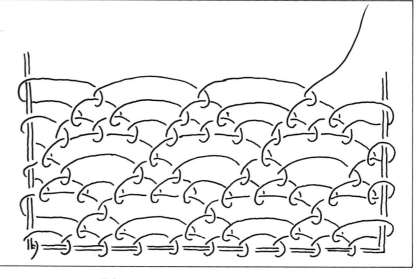

●●● NEEDLELACE FAN

This pattern imitates tape lace in its design. Work in 50 DMC Broder Machine. Follow the general instructions for needlelace (p. 78).

Work corded Brussels in **1**, Double Brussels in **2**, Pea stitch in **3**, Pyramid stitch in **4** (see instructions p. 78) and spider wheels and bars where indicated. Work a series of buttonhole loops on top of one another to form peaks on the outer edge.

MOUNTING FANS

Spread the sticks to fit the lace and paint them with white PVA woodworking glue. Attach the lace and allow to dry. This glue dries transparent.

5.9

6
PARASOLS

Parasols came into use during the Regency period and were particularly fashionable among the Victorians. It was considered that the sun harmed the skin and the face should be shielded to maintain a delicate complexion. The parasol thus became a necessary accessory. It was made using all forms of lace.

Small folding parasol frames are available in plastic, but these have rather ugly handles.

The handles can, however, be removed and replaced with a wooden handle. You will find that a chopstick is about the right length and width.

Most parasols are not quite a circle, so that they form a domed shape when mounted. Some of the following patterns are complete circles because of the design, but the parasol frames adjust to this.

●● BUTTERFLY PARASOL

40 pairs 50 DMC Broder Machine, 1 pair gimp DMC 12 perlé

Work using the Torchon or Bucks Point technique on a curved ground. The pricking can be reduced to 70% for ¹/₁₂ scale. Work in 160 Brok. This pattern, which slightly domed, makes a small parasol. For a larger one a lace frill can be added (p. 82). The butterflies are worked as in fig. 1.19 and the shell edge as in p. 47. Start at **A** with three pairs and add pairs from **A** to **B**, two pairs at each pin hole. Carry the gimp along from one butterfly to the next. The trail that separates the outer edge and the centre accommodates the change in ground size. Leave ends for sewing from **D** to **E** and join to **AC**.

ALTERNATIVE METHODS FOR WORKING THE PARASOL

The outer butterfly edge **A** to **B** can be used on its own or made separately and attached to the centre part with sewings. An alternative centre can also be used, worked in Torchon or rose ground. This can be combined with the fan patterns in figs 5.1 or 5.2 (p. 69 and 72).

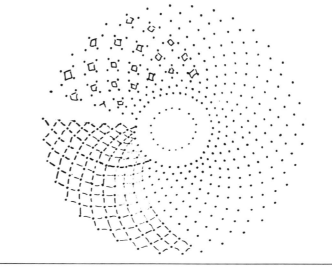

6.1

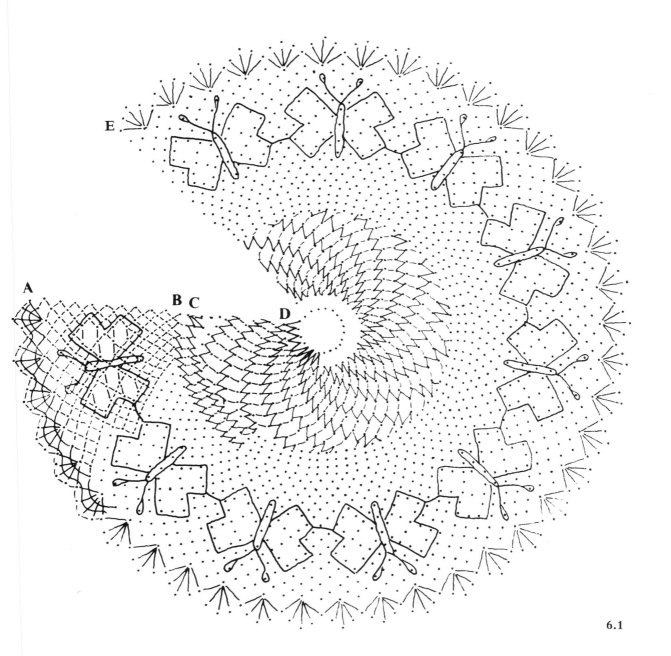

6.1

Three parasols. Top: Bucks Point parasol (fig. 6.2); left: petalled parasol (fig. 6.3); right: needlelace parasol (fig. 6.6)

Opposite: Detail of butterfly parasol shown in photograph on p. 15 (fig. 6.1)

Detail of Bucks Point parasol (fig. 6.2)

●●● BUCKS FLORAL PARASOL

49 pairs 50 or 60 Brok, 5 pairs gimp DMC 12 perlé

This is a domed shape, using the Bucks hexagon technique with five segments worked.

Begin at **A** and work in the direction shown; add pairs to **B**. Complete the segment **ABC**. Work cloth stitch in the leaves and make the flowers as in fig. 1.8. Turn the pillow and work the next segment **CBD**. Repeat for **DBE**, **EBF** and **FBG**. When complete join **GB** to **AB**. Overlap the honeycomb ring at **G** with **A**.

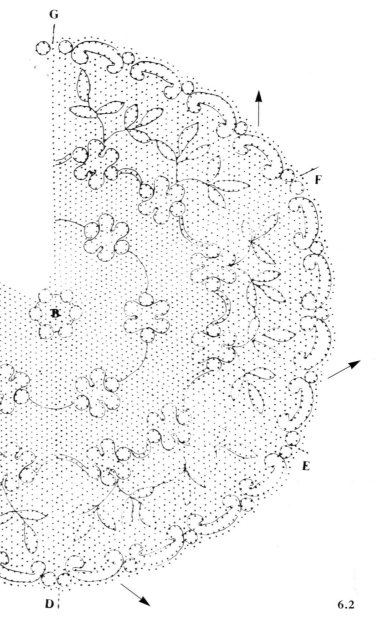

6.2

●●● PETALLED PARASOL

22 pairs 60 Brok, 1 pair gimp
DMC 12 perlé (centre)
35 pairs 60 Brok, 1 pair gimp
DMC 12 perlé (outer edge)

This is domed and is designed to fit the eight sections of the parasol frame. Each flower coincides with a strut. Work the part inner circle first from **A** to **B** and leave the thread ends to sew in later. The full circle pricking is useful for a

doll's house cloth. Mark out one edge pattern and reverse it for the second so that the patterns follow on. Fit to the inner circle and follow the diagram, sewing into the centre where they meet. Pairs accumulate on the pointed edge as shown; follow fig. 6.3 for the position of the pins.

The crossed trails vary in size. Cross in the usual way, making sure that the correct number are in each trail at the end of the procedure.

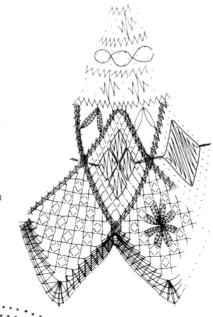

6.3

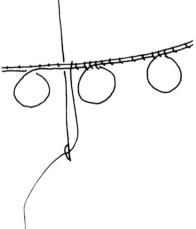

Carrickmacross parasol (fig. 6.4)

Traditional Carrickmacross looped edge

Detail of petalled parasol (fig. 6.3)

●● CARRICKMACROSS SPRAYS

Six segments make a skirt for a $\frac{1}{12}$ scale doll. Mark out eight segments so that a part circle is formed and follow the general instructions for Carrickmacross (p. 33).

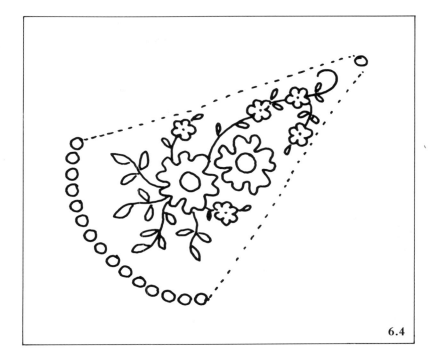

6.4

Detail of needlelace parasol (fig. 6.6)

● **CARRICKMACROSS FLOWERS**

These can be used to make a complete circle, which will fit a fully extended parasol. Trace off and proceed as for general Carrickmacross. The edge can be buttonholed, or worked in Point de Venise. Alternatively, use a traditional edging as in the fig. 6.4. Colour can be added by darning through the net under the flowers and leaves on the reverse side (see the photograph on p. 90).

6.5

●●● NEEDLELACE PARASOL

Follow the general instructions for needlelace (p. 28). Work in Brok 36 or 30 DMC Broder Machine.

Work Corded Brussels in **1**, Double Brussels in **2**, pea stitch in **3**, woven wheels in **4**, worked bars in **5** (the central area) and crossed worked bars on the outer edge.

Attach net to the outer area **6** before the final top buttonhole stitching. Work over two threads and the net, and trim away the surplus.

6.6

Carrickmacross parasol (fig. 6.5), showing darning on the net behind in mauve and green

MAKING UP A PARASOL LINING

Cut eight segments as in fig. 6.4 and pink the curved edge. Seam these together with small running stitches, leaving a small hole at the top. Make another eight segments for the inner lining.

Push the inner lining over the handle and attach at the points where the folding struts begin and at the outer edge. Place the top lining over the centre and attach at the outer edges of the frame.

Place the lace over the top and lightly sew into place.

7
VEILS AND SHAWLS

Veils and shawls were at the height of their popularity in the Victorian era. Bonnet veils were among the most popular. These were very large, covering the face, and long enough to be thrown back over the bonnet and left to hang down the back. Victorian veils often had deep lace edges. They were worn at weddings, and the fashion for covering the face before the wedding ceremony seems to have appeared in the late nineteenth century. Lace shawls, particularly Chantilly and Blonde, were worn to most evening functions. They were often in black because the pale-coloured evening dresses showed the lace patterning off to perfection.

Detail of Limerick veil (fig. 7.2)

A

B

7.1

●●●● CHANTILLY SHAWL

200 pairs approx. worked in 100 Brok or 80 Madeira black. Many gimps in 30 DMC Broder Machine

This is a difficult pattern and should only be attempted by experienced lacemakers.
Join the pieces together to form a triangle, **AB** to **AB** on either side of the centre. Working instructions for a piece such as this are almost impossible to give, but experienced Bucks workers will find it quite straightforward to work. Work in half stitch for black and cloth stitch for cream.

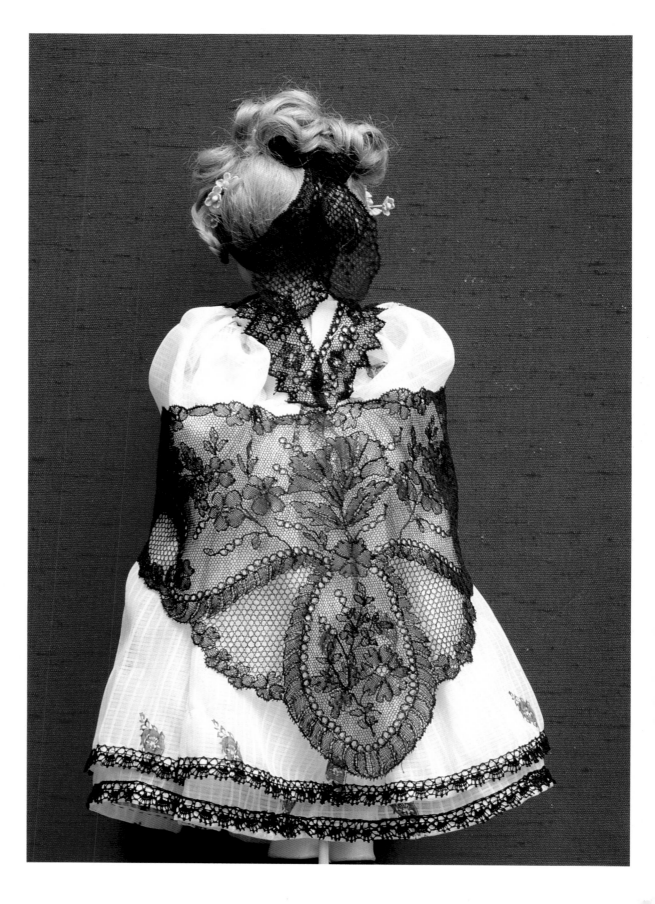

●●●● **LIMERICK VEIL**

MATERIALS REQUIRED

75 cm. (30 in.) square tulle
Embroidery frame
Stranded cotton
50 to 60 silk thread

(enlarge patterns by 250%)
If you are new to this form of fine
embroidery, work a small spray
first. Attach net to frame so that
the net ground lies in a north/south,
east/west direction when under
tension. Trace off the entire veil
pattern, four corners and four
sides. Check that you have a
perfect square. Use an indelible
pen and place the drawing under
the net, reverse side uppermost so
that the pen does not touch the
net. Tack firmly into position with
a fine thread, taking care not to
damage the tulle.

Using one strand of stranded
thread, darn in and out of the net
holes, following the drawing
underneath. It is sometimes
necessary to go over two holes to
keep the continuity of the design.
Use long lengths of thread and if a
join is needed run the thread
alongside for a short distance. Try
to make the line as continuous as
possible. When all the outlining is
complete, take away the drawing
and work the fillings with the fine
silk thread.

Use plain darning in the small
scrolls and in **0**, zigzag darning in
1, cobweb stitch in **2** and wave
stitch in **3**. Finally buttonhole the
outer edge and cut away the
surplus net.

Opposite: *Back view of evening dress
in photograph on p. 2, showing the
Chantilly shawl (fig. 7.1) and lappets
(figs. 2.7) worked in black*

7.2

LIMERICK FILLINGS

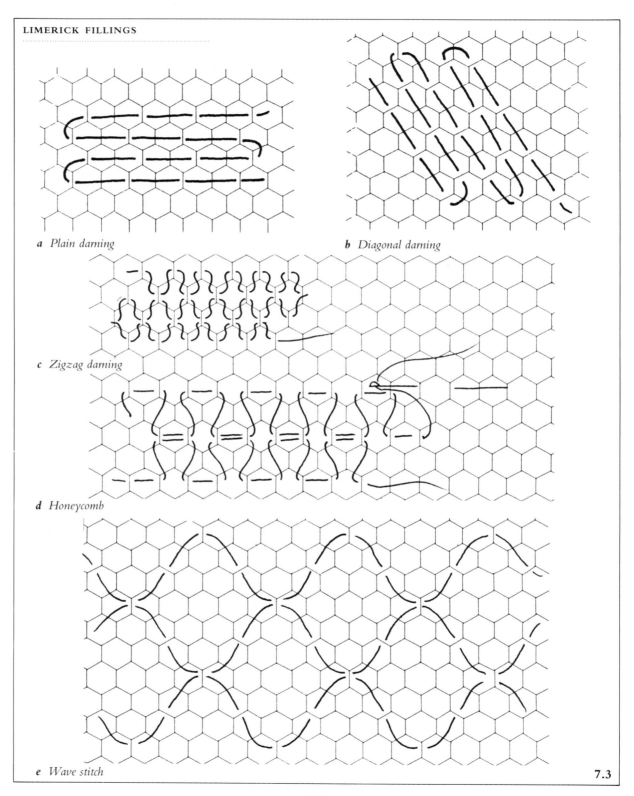

a Plain darning

b Diagonal darning

c Zigzag darning

d Honeycomb

e Wave stitch

7.3

8
DRESSING DOLLS

Dolls can be purchased in kit form with a porcelain head and limbs and a soft body. Patterns are also available for dolls' clothes in various period styles, but these are not always accurate. In the past, dresses were designed to fit the fashionable silhouette, which may make the patterns unsuitable for modern dolls. The patterns in this chapter are as authentic as possible, given that one is working in quarter scale.

MAKING COSTUME DOLLS

- Make the doll's body soft round the waist so that it can be corseted.
- Always make a corset as this gives shape to the figure when dressed.
- Wire the arms so that the doll can be posed with a fan or parasol. Take wire from one arm to the other, making a loop in the body to stop it moving.
- Sew through the knee-line and hip-line if you want the doll to be seated.
- Use a tubular finger bandage for stockings, and small-patterned or plain material for dresses, with fine lawn for underwear.
- Prior to 1860, the sewing machine had not been invented, so dresses should be handsewn for maximum authenticity.

USING THE PATTERNS

Cut patterns out of a soft paper towel first, pin together and make any necessary adjustments. Patterns can be reduced or enlarged to fit different-sized dolls. The symbol ↔ indicates the straight of the grain.

All patterns have ½ cm. (¼ in.) turnings allowed. Use very soft, iron-on Vilene on bodices; this makes them easier to handle, and only single turnings will be necessary for the edges. Always sew the bodice, shoulder seams and darts first. Sew in the sleeve head and then sew the side seams of the bodice and the sleeve seams at the same time.

Useful trimmings can be made by working long lengths of crossway, folding edges to the middle and running a gathering thread through the centre, catching in the folded edges. Pleated frills make a good decoration at the hemline. Pink both edges before pleating.

Small round beads with worked loops make good front fastenings. Use small hooks and worked bars for a back opening.

Make petticoats, chemises and pantaloons with draw-strings; this eliminates the need for openings and makes the material easier to gather.

For patterns see pp. 104–22.

UNDERCLOTHES

Underclothes were trimmed either with bobbin lace, needle-point lace or broderie anglaise. It was usual to wear a chemise under a corset, and short or long pantaloons with one or more petticoats.

THE CORSET

A satisfactory corset can be made in stiff Vilene. Make darts where indicated and sew Rigilene (available from most haberdashers') in strips over each dart and either side of the centre back. Fold the back edge over the Rigilene and thread fine ribbon or cord through to lace the doll tight. If threaded through a large needle the cord or ribbon can be pulled through the Rigilene without having to make extra holes. Place on the doll first and lace into position; no turnings are needed.

Alternatively, stiff iron-on Vilene can be used with a fancy material and the corset trimmed with lace. Add a ½ cm. (¼ in.) turning to the pattern, and make small hems top and bottom.

CHEMISE

This is worn underneath the corset. The back and front are the same; the body and sleeve length should be adjusted before cutting out. Join the shoulders with French seams and make a small rolled hem at the neckline and sleeve edges. Attach lace to these and run a gathering thread on the dotted line to pull up the sleeve and neck to fit the doll. This will allow for a high or low neckline. Make a 1 cm. (½ in.) hem at the bottom.

Opposite: *Lady, 1890s. Dress features collar made from a circle of lace (fig. 5.1), worn with a Chantilly shawl (fig. 7.1)*

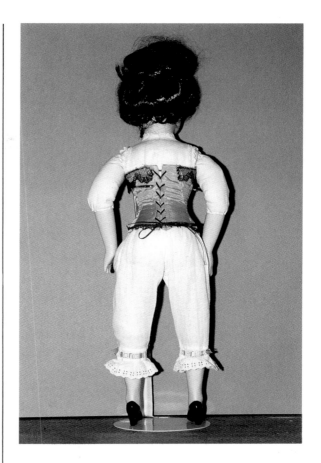

Corset showing lacing with ribbon and lace trim (fig. 8.1)

PANTALOONS

These are made as two separate legs with a split round the crutch. Cut out in lawn, either full length, or cut off at the dotted line with a small frill added at the knee. Make each leg separately with a small hem from waist to crutch. Make a 1 cm. (½ in.) hem at the waist and thread a cord through. Pull this up to fit the doll's waist under the corset.

PETTICOATS

These are usually made from straight pieces of material; 68 cm. (27 in.) is adequate (less under narrow dresses). The top can be gathered into a waistband, but I have found that by making a narrow hem at the top and inserting a draw-string, the gathers can be adjusted to suit the style of the dress. There is thus no need for an opening. The hemline can be decorated with embroidery, tucks, insets and lace.

HISTORICAL DRESS

STUART

See photographs on pp. 31 and 58. This period in history saw the lavish use of lace on both male and female clothing. Lace was very expensive and to wear it was a sign of wealth. Bobbin and needlepoint lace were both used, and some of the finest was often smuggled into Britain from the Continent. Men wore lace collars and cuffs, as well as lace tops to their boots and rosettes on their shoes. They often carried large lace-edged kerchiefs. Women wore deep lace collars and cuffs, often attached to lawn.

Underclothes for women consisted of a lace-trimmed chemise, petticoat and corset but there is no mention of underpants. Dresses were made from plain materials (often embroidered), taffeta, silk, satin and velvet, in reds, pinks, mauves, green, blue and plum.

Petticoats should be made 68 cm. (27 in.) wide and ankle length. Make a small hem at the top and thread ribbon or cord through; pull up to fit waist. Gathers should be adjusted towards the back and side.

THE LADY

Cut out bodice sections **A**, **B** and **C** and hand-sew the back and side seams. Make the shoulder seams. Gather the top of the sleeve and attach to the armhole, matching the notches. Sew side and sleeve seams. Make a small hem at the front edge and round the lower edge. Make the busk by sewing round two pieces of material plus Vilene, leaving a small gap at the top to turn through to the right side. Make the cuffs by joining into a tube and seaming the outer edge; turn through and sew to the sleeve ends, attaching lace to the top edge. Make the collar and attach this to the neck edge. Add lace to the collar and top of the busk. The busk is separate and the front edge of the dress pins to it. The dress skirt is cut as a half-circle with a hole cut out to fit the waist. This is worn separately from the bodice.

THE CAVALIER

Use the pantaloon pattern cut to the knee for the trousers but join at the crutch. Gather the top with a cord and make a small hem at the bottom of each leg. Use the chemise pattern for the shirt, extending the sleeve and bottom. The sleeve needs to be extra long so that it can puff out in the jacket sleeve splits. Gather the sleeve to a small cuff and gather the neck up to fit the lace collar; it will be necessary to make a small front opening.

Sew the jacket body seams, leaving open where indicated. Make the dart in the sleeve and leave the sleeve seam open. Attach the sleeve to the jacket, easing the top. Make small turnings at the neckline, centre front, split seams and the bottom of the jacket and sleeves. Trim with a narrow braid where indicated. This outfit can also be used for the Victorian boy in the photograph on p. 54. Add a turning to the front jacket with buttons and loops, and gather legs into a band.

REGENCY (1800–20)

See photographs on pp. 7 and 35. Early in the nineteenth century, dresses were narrow and lace was very light and open. Machine net had now been invented, and embroidery was also used for decoration. Dresses were often made from fine lawn or muslin, revealing the figure, so underclothes were very important. Pantaloons to the ankle became essential.

Dresses increased in width by 1815 with long sleeves and high frilled necklines. Parasols and fans were very fashionable and large hats were worn with veils. For outer wear, the 'Spencer' jacket was worn, made from a heavier material than the dress. Later this was extended to make a long coat called a pelisse, which was decorated at the hemline. Transparent fabrics were used in pale colours, cream and white in the early Regency period, with spotted and flowered materials coming into fashion later.

EARLY REGENCY LADY

The bodice comes just below the bust and can be darted or gathered. The dotted line indicates a deep neckline. The shoulder seam lies well to the back. The line **ab** is normally a seam — you will find it easier to make a very small dart. Join the shoulder seams, and gather the sleeve to fit the armhole. Sew into place and then sew side and sleeve seams. The narrow skirt is cut in a straight piece to the ankle (41 cm./16 in. minimum). Attach this to the bodice and leave a small opening. Fasten with small hooks and worked bars.

Underclothes Make the petticoat (the same size as the skirt), long pantaloons, and a chemise with a low neckline. There is no corset.

MID-REGENCY LADY

See photograph on p. 35. Make the bodice as for the early Regency dress. The sleeves, however, are longer than in the previous pattern. Attach **C** and **D** before cutting out. Cut the skirt slightly wider (51 cm./20 in.).

The Spencer Jacket Make the bodice as for the early Regency dress. Gather the puff sleeve **E** to fit the armhole, and the lower edge of the sleeve to fit **D**. Sew the sleeve head into the armhole and then complete the bodice side seams and the sleeve seam. A frill of lace or net can be added to the neckline and the sleeve bottoms. Fasten with worked loops and beads for buttons.

LATE REGENCY TO EARLY VICTORIAN (1820–40)

See photographs on pp. 11 and 39. The narrow dresses of the Regency period increased in width and the waistline gradually dropped. Sleeves were larger, and were known as gigots. Large lace collars were also fashionable. As waists became more pronounced, the corset was worn once more, and was very tightly laced. Pantaloons, worn to the ankle, were lavishly trimmed with lace and embroidery, as was the chemise. Petticoats were as full as the skirts, with corded pin-tucks to make them stand out at the hem. The fullness was to the sides and back, with a padded 'bum roll' to accentuate the shape. This was tied round the waist.

Children of this period were still dressed as adults, but girls wore knee-length skirts until about the age of twelve, when the hem became calf-length. By the age of sixteen, full-length skirts were worn. Boys were dressed as girls until they were 'breached' at about six years old.

The christening robe that we know today was introduced in this period, with a pointed waist for girls and a straight waist for boys. These were sold in kit form.

The materials used were gingham, chintz and other printed fabrics, with voile, made of silk, cotton or wool, for evening wear.

EVENING DRESS (1830)

See photographs on pp. 2 and 39. Make darts and sew shoulder seams. Use the puff sleeve from the mid-Regency dress or a gigot sleeve, and gather sleeve head to fit armhole. Sew side and sleeve seams. Lace can be added to the puff sleeve and the bottom gathered to fit the arm. A lace plastron can also be worn. The skirt is a straight length of material 75 cm. (30 in.) wide, opening at centre back. It can be separate from the bodice with a small waistband.

DAY DRESS (1830)

The neck of the chemise can be drawn up to fill the deep neckline of the evening bodice; small gigot sleeves can be worn with lace cuffs and a pelerine collar. Make a skirt as for the evening dress.

The pelerine collar is lace edged, requiring 66 cm. (26 in.) of edging. Make a collar in single thickness organdie or lawn. Sew a 1 cm. (¼ in.) rolled hem from the front neck, down centre front and round the neck. Attach the lace to this, gathering slightly on the points and curves.

The underclothes consist of corsets, long pantaloons, a petticoat and a chemise.

EARLY TO MID-VICTORIAN (1840–60)

Dresses now became wider and were gathered very tightly, worn at first over several petticoats. Sleeves became narrow and the bodice shoulders sloped so that sleeves were set in lower. Waists were reduced in size by the use of very tight corsets. Lace was used on fans and folding carriage parasols.

The invention of the crinoline in about 1850 meant that the skirt could be widened more easily, and was lighter to wear. The skirt formed a bell shape and was often in several tiers. However, it became far too wide and unmanageable, and laws were passed preventing factory workers from wearing it. Jackets with 'lantern' sleeves were fashionable at this time, with undersleeves of lace and lawn. Necklines were high except for evening wear, and the small, round collar was popular. The Chantilly shawl was worn only by wealthy women. The patterning of the black lace showed up to perfection against the pale-coloured evening dresses.

DRESS (1850)

See photograph on p. 27. This pattern has a back opening but if the front is placed to the fold and a 1½ cm. (½ in.) turning added, it can be used with buttons and loops at the front.

Make darts and sew shoulder seams. Gather sleeve head and sew into armhole. Sew side and sleeve seams. Make small hems at the sleeve, neck, back and bottom edges of the bodice. Make a separate skirt in a straight piece 75 cm. (30 in.) long. This can be cut in two tiers, one full length and one three-quarter length, gathered together in a waistband.

The jacket is worn instead of the bodice. Make the back by darting the side back at the waistline and joining to the back. Make darts at the front, sew the shoulder seams and ease in the lantern sleeve head. Sew side and sleeve seams. Make small hems at the edge of the sleeve, the neckline and at the bottom of the jacket.

This is worn with a small, round collar and undersleeves. Narrow braid can be added to the bottom of the sleeve to give weight. The jacket can be fully lined by cutting another in a light material and joining at the bottom and sleeve edges, although this will make it more bulky.

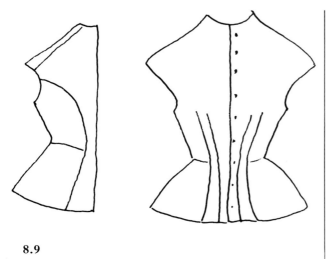

8.9

The undryclothes consist of a corset, chemise, calf-length pantaloons and petticoat. A crinoline petticoat can be made by cutting a straight length of lawn, and gathering it to fit a waistband. Rigilene stitch round the hemline and 5 cm (1½ in.) above the hemline.

LATER VICTORIAN (1870–80)

The crinoline gave way to the bustle at this time. A cage was placed under the petticoat at the back and tied into place. The dress was draped over this. Pleating was often used at the lower ege of the skirt, with ribbon and lace trimmings. The emphasis was at the back of the dress. Bodice and skirt were still separate, with high necklines worn by day, and very low ones in the evening.

WEDDING DRESS

See photograph, p. 70. Seam the centre back, make darts, and sew the shoulder seams. Gather the sleeve head and sew into place. Make the side and sleeve seams. Make a small hem round the neckline, sleeve edges and centre front. Fit the peplum, pleating it around the waist. Make a small hem at centre fronts and bottom edge of peplum. Lace can be added to this if desired. Sew a double frill (see fig. 4.3) round neck and sleeve edges. Add a ruffle to the sleeve.

Make a skirt 92 cm. (36 in.) wide. This skirt should be ankle-length and 5 cm. (2 in.) deeper at the back to accommodate the bustle. Make a hem at the top and bottom and put a draw-string in the top. Pull this up to fit the waist, placing the gathers at the back. Make a pleated frill for the lower edge.

EVENING DRESS

See photograph on p. 46. Make up as for the wedding dress, but use the puffed sleeve from the mid-Regency pattern on p. 113 and add a Bertha collar (see fig. 4.4) to the low neckline. A net or lace overskirt can be added also.

The underclothes consist of a corset, chemise, calf-length pantaloons and petticoat. Make a padded cushion to tie round the waist to form a bustle; adjust the size to suit the doll.

THE 1890s

Dresses became narrower at the end of Queen Victoria's reign. There was still a small bustle, and the front skirt was tied behind with tapes to keep it tight. The back of the dress was the most important feature. Evening dresses had a train which swept the floor and was carried over the arm when walking or dancing.

The train gradually disappeared as women became more emancipated, and by the end of the century, skirts were gored and ankle length. The sleeves became larger like the gigot sleeves of the mid-Victorian period, but were cut in a slightly different way and known as the 'leg of mutton'. The waist was corseted firmly to give an hour-glass look. Lace was still widely used and machine lace was available for the first time. Hand-made lace was very expensive and worn only by the most wealthy. Heavy Venetian lace was again popular.

Little girls now had far more freedom to play. They no longer wore restrictive corsets, or dresses with tight waists, although they often had white aprons to keep their clothes clean.

DAY DRESS (1894)

See photographs on p. 66. Sew the darts in the bodice and bone with Rigilene. Bone at centre front and turn back the edge. Sew shoulder seams and insert the gathered sleeve head. Sew side and sleeve seams. Make a hem at the bottom of the sleeve and add the lace before gathering to fit the arm.

Join the top sleeve to the narrow sleeve pattern of the early Regency dress (p. 113) to make a long sleeve. This can be worn with a narrow cuff. Make a small hem at the bottom of the bodice and fasten to centre front with hooks and worked bars, or with worked loops and bead buttons.

The skirt is a quarter circle, with the centre cut out to fit the waistline; it is divided into four gores.

The underclothes consist of a petticoat, cut to a quarter-circle and frilled at the hemline, a corset, and a chemise with knee-length pantaloons decorated with frills of lace or broderie anglaise.

GRAPHS FOR ACCESSORIES

8.13 Useful quarter-circle curved graphs for fans, parasols and collars

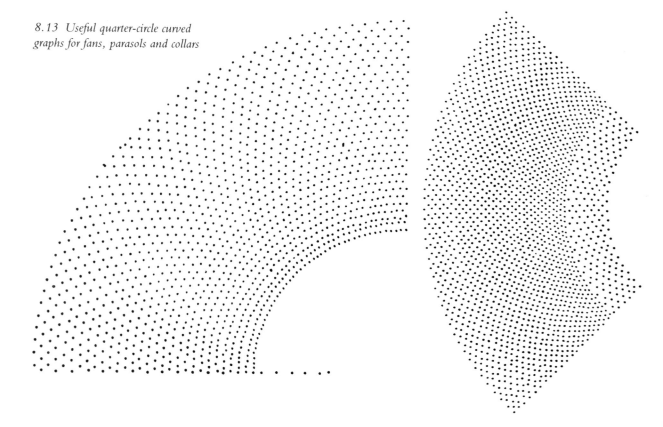

THE PATTERNS

Trace the pattern and cut out in soft paper towel. Pin darts and seams. Try underclothes on a naked doll. Try all dress patterns over corset and underclothes. Make any necessary adjustments to the pattern before cutting out in the final material. These patterns fit 16–18 in. dolls but can be enlarged or reduced for 24 in. and $1/12$ scale. Choose soft, lightweight material in plain colours or with a small design.

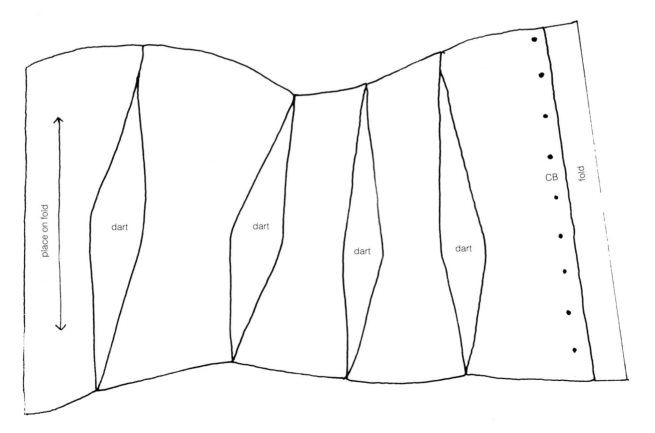

8.1 Corset as in fig. 63 (see photograph, p. 99)

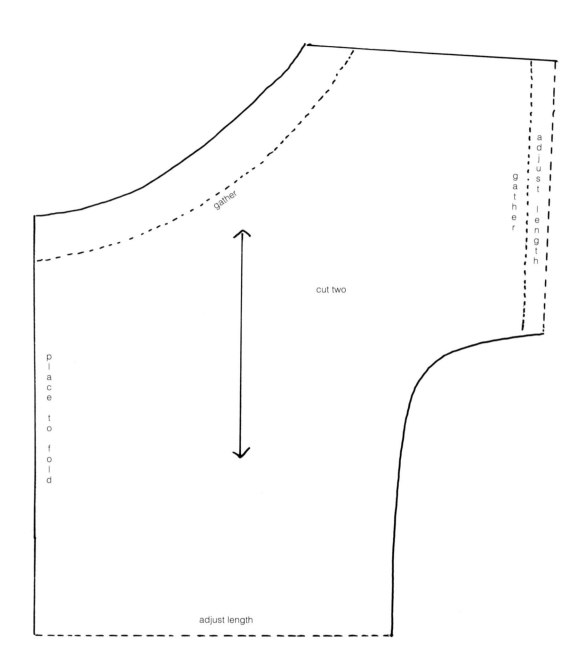

gather

cut two

place to fold

adjust length

gather

adjust length

adjust length

8.2 *Chemise*

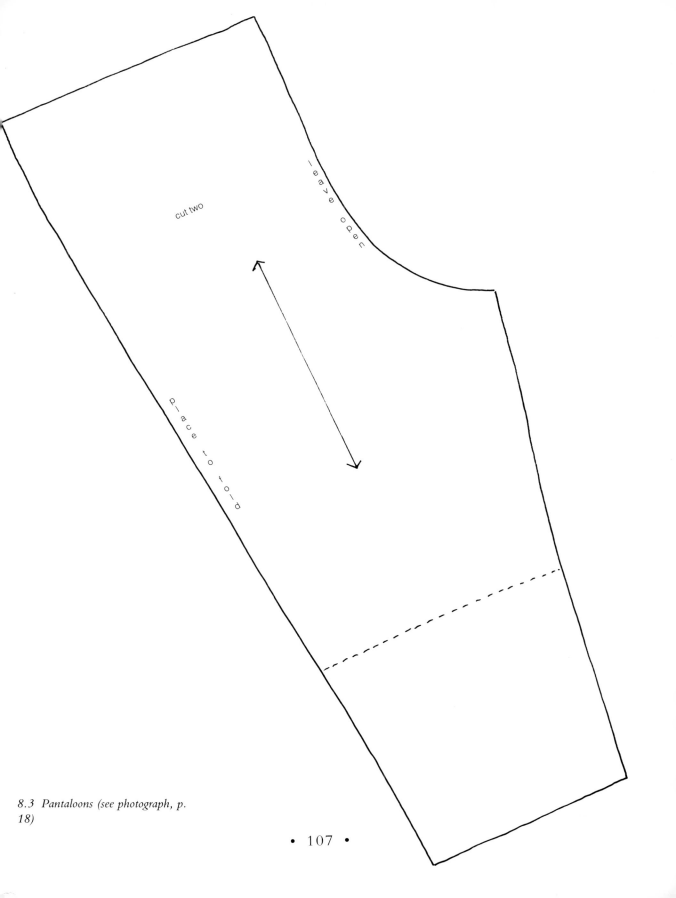

cut two

leave open

place to fold

8.3 Pantaloons (see photograph, p. 18)

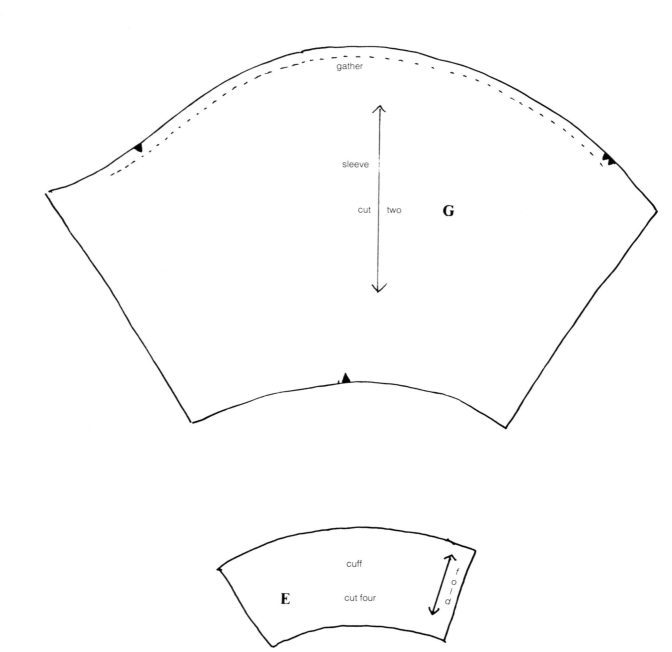

gather

sleeve

cut   two   **G**

cuff

E   cut four   fold

8.4 *Stuart lady*

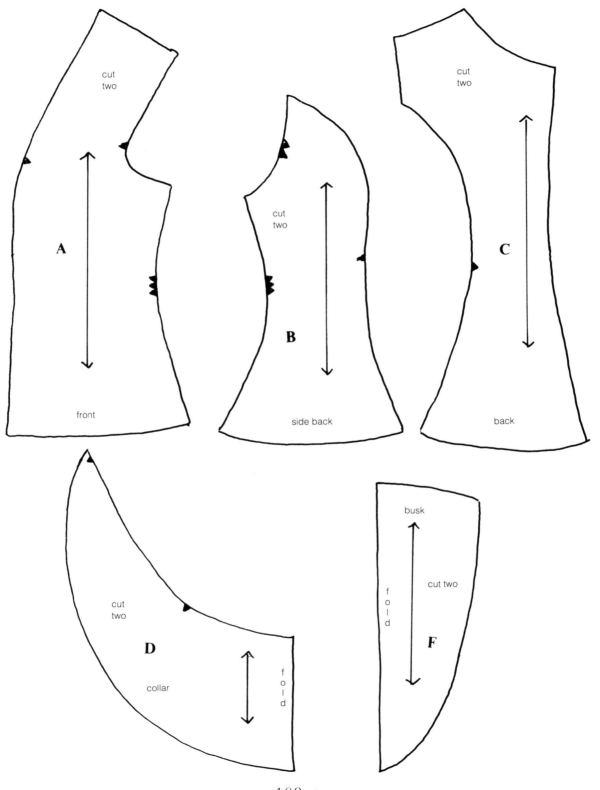

cut
two

A

front

cut
two

B

side back

cut
two

C

back

cut
two

D

collar

fold

busk

fold

cut two

F

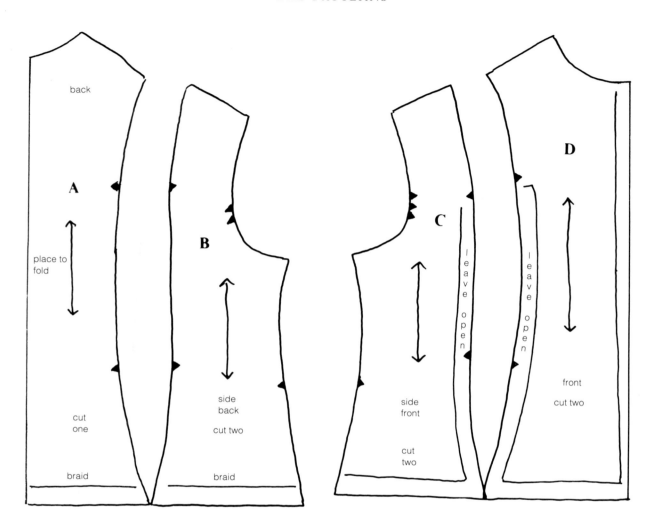

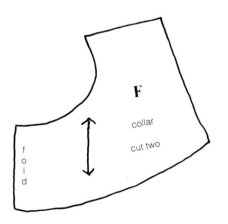

8.5 Cavalier (see photograph, p. 58)

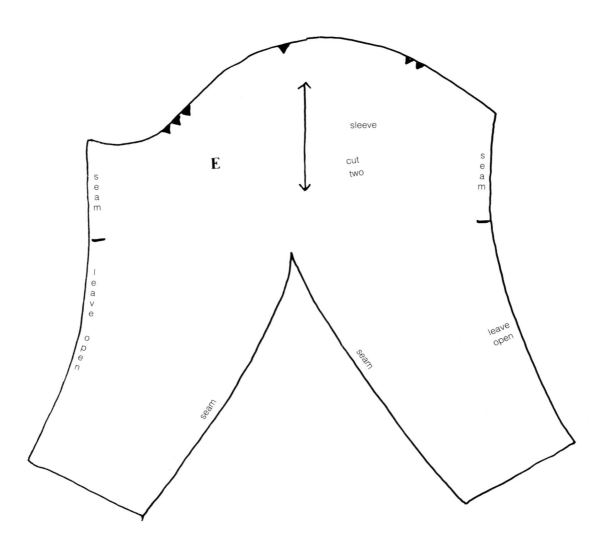

E

sleeve

cut
two

seam

seam

seam

seam

leave
open

leave
open

seam

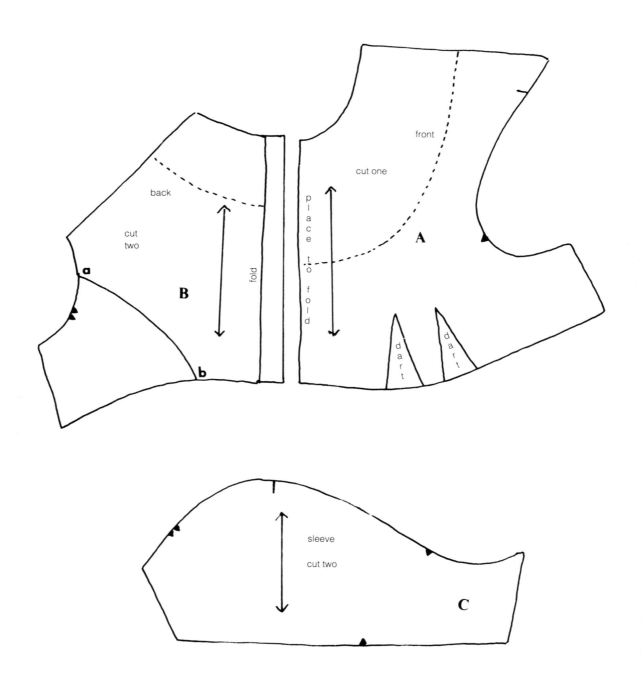

back

cut
two

cut one

front

B

A

fold

place to fold

dart

dart

a

b

sleeve

cut two

C

8.6 Early Regency lady (see photographs, pp. 7, 34 and 35)

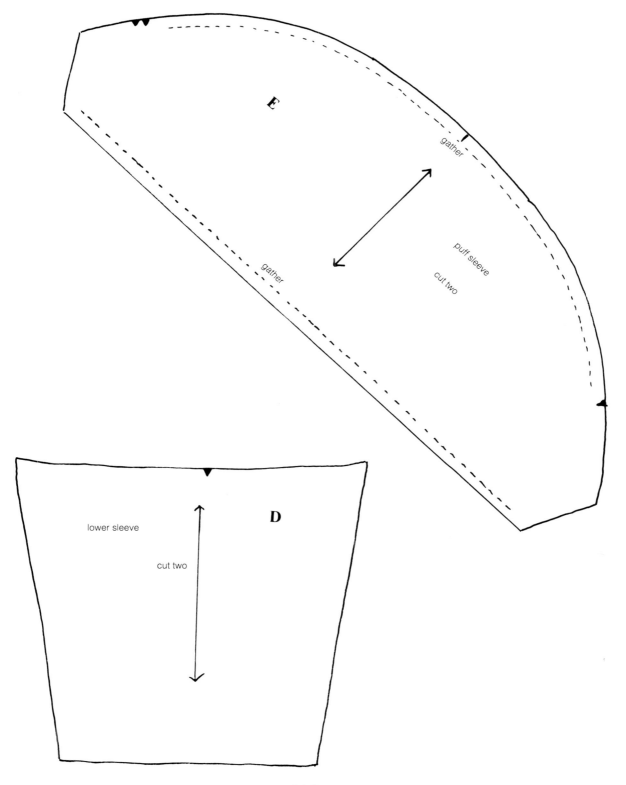

E

gather

gather

puff sleeve

cut two

lower sleeve

D

cut two

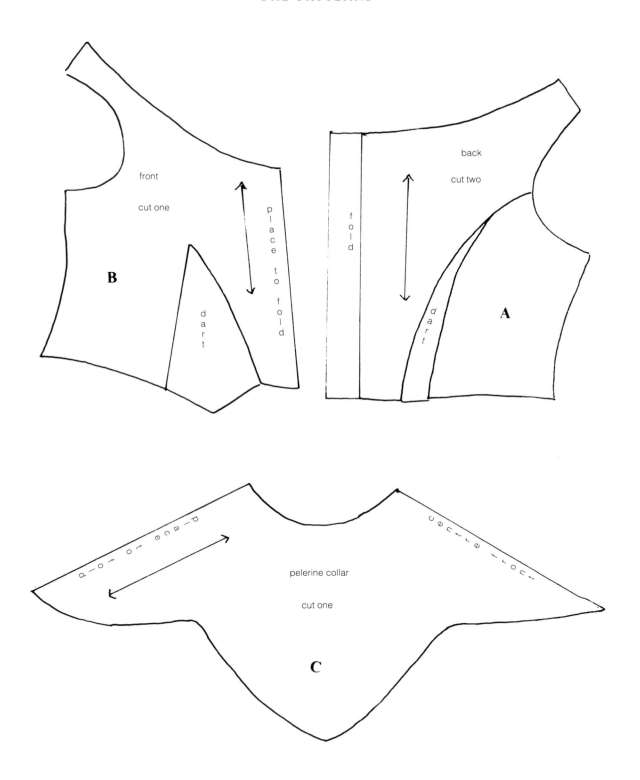

front

cut one

B

place to fold

dart

back

cut two

fold

dart

A

pelerine collar

cut one

place to fold

centre front

C

8.7 Early Victorian lady (see photographs, pp. 11, 39 and 2)

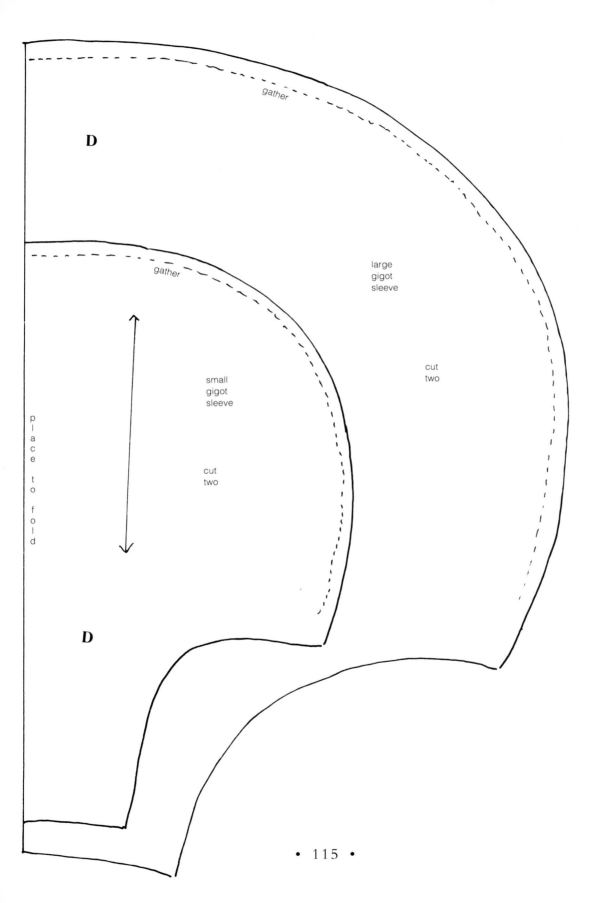

D

gather

large
gigot
sleeve

cut
two

gather

small
gigot
sleeve

cut
two

place to fold

D

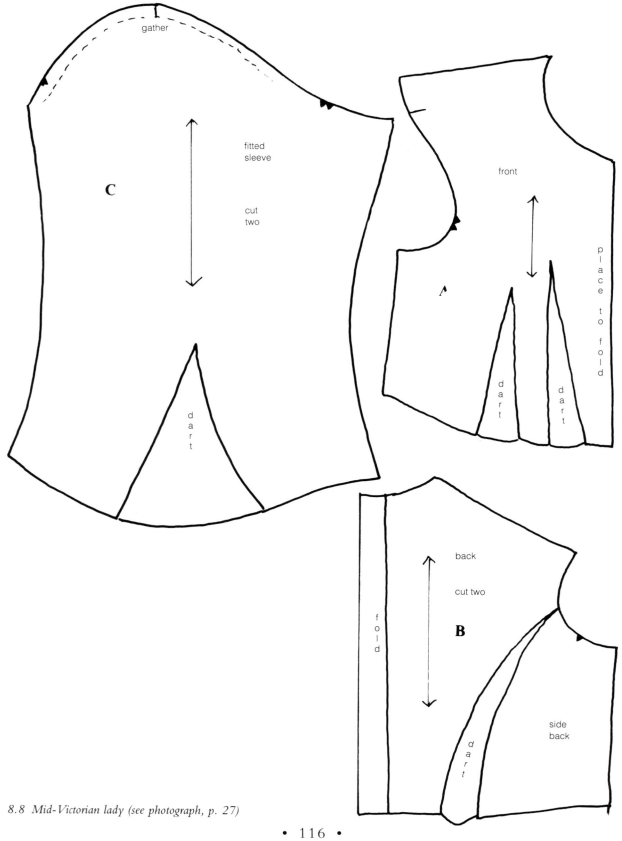

gather

fitted
sleeve

C

cut
two

d
a
r
t

front

place to fold

d
a
r
t

d
a
r
t

back

cut two

f
o
l
d

B

d
a
r
t

side
back

8.8 Mid-Victorian lady (see photograph, p. 27)

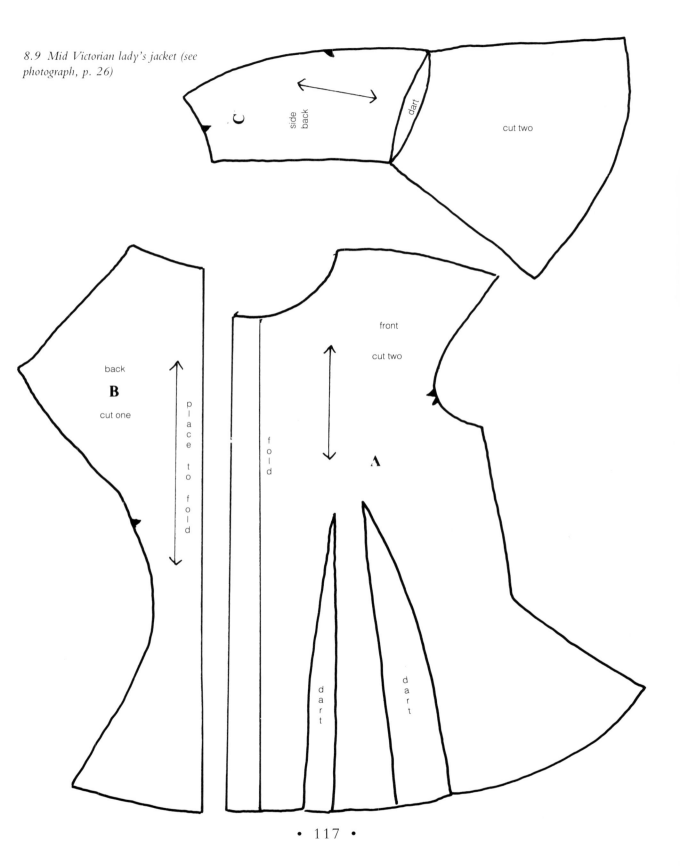

8.9 Mid Victorian lady's jacket (see photograph, p. 26)

C

side back

dart

cut two

back

B

cut one

place to fold

front

cut two

fold

A

dart

dart

8.9

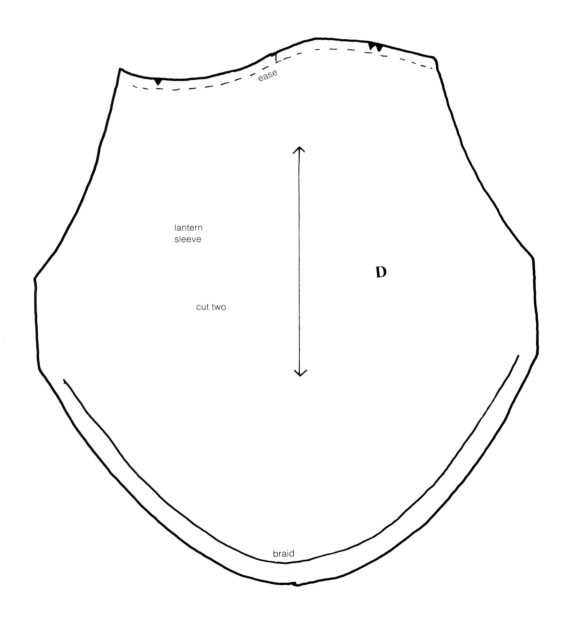

ease

lantern
sleeve

cut two

D

braid

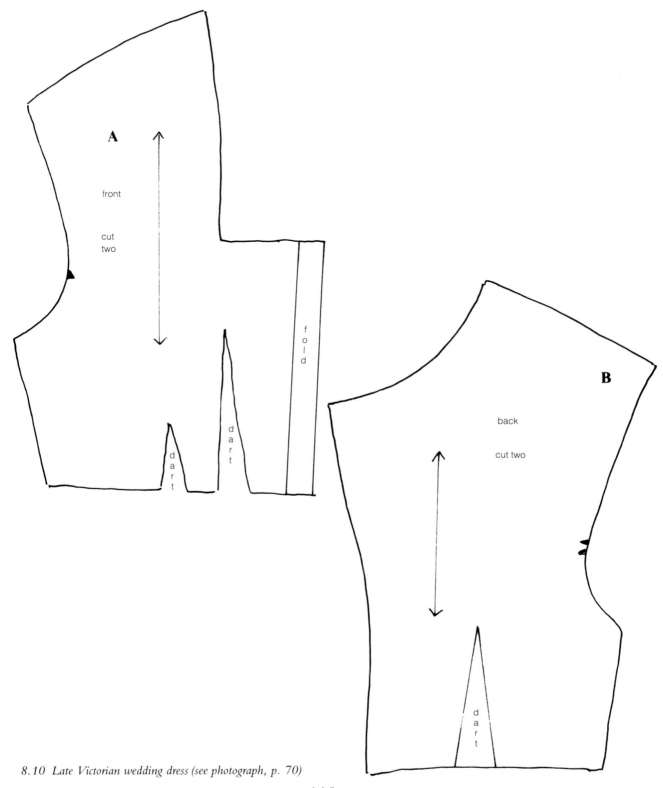

A

front

cut
two

d a r t

d a r t

f o l d

B

back

cut two

d a r t

8.10 Late Victorian wedding dress (see photograph, p. 70)

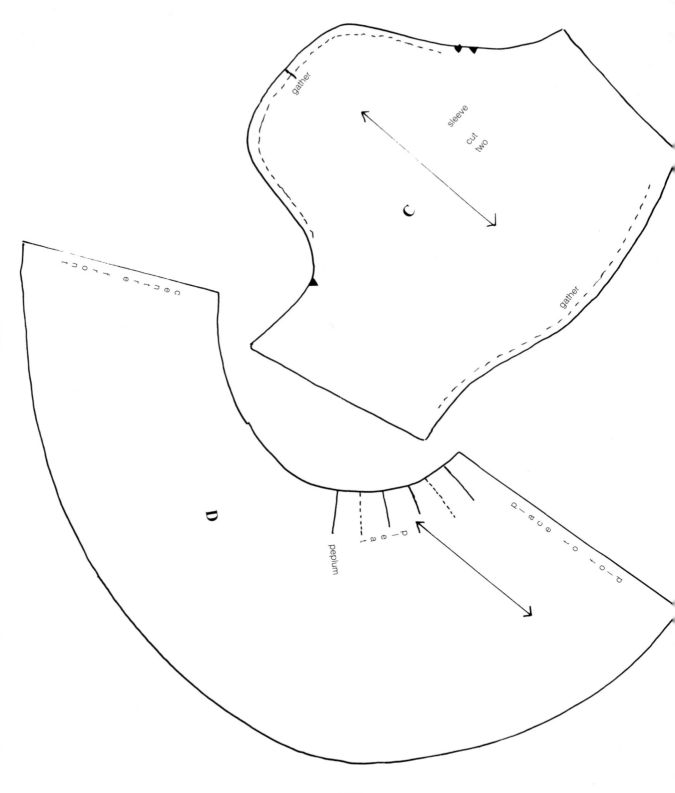

THE PATTERNS

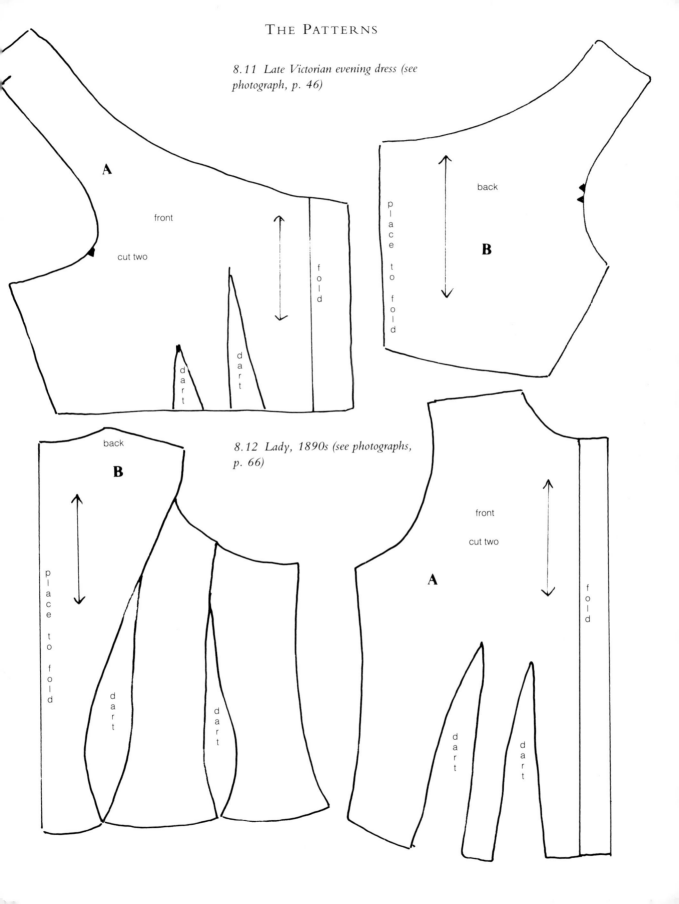

8.11 Late Victorian evening dress (see photograph, p. 46)

A

front

cut two

dart

dart

fold

B

back

place to fold

8.12 Lady, 1890s (see photographs, p. 66)

B

back

place to fold

dart

dart

A

front

cut two

dart

dart

fold

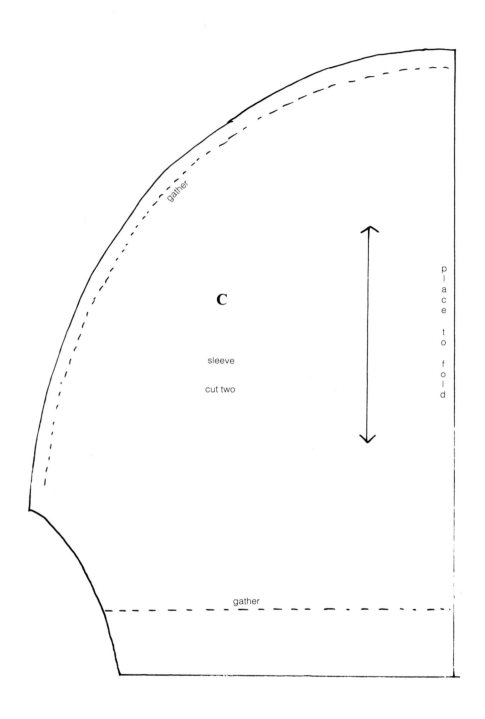

C

sleeve

cut two

gather

gather

place to fold

FURTHER READING

Atkinson, Sue, *Making and Dressing Doll's House Dolls in Twelve-Scale*, David and Charles (1992)

Arnold, Janet, *Patterns of Fashion, 1660–1860* Wace & Co.

— *Patterns of Fashion, 1860–1940*, Wace and Co.

Courtais, Georgine de, *Women's Head-dress and Hair Styles*, Batsford (1973)

Desmonde, Kay, *Dolls*, Octopus Books (1974)

Earnshaw, Pat, *Lace in Fashion*, Batsford (1985)

Ewing, Elizabeth, *Everyday Dress, 1650–1900*, Batsford (1984)

Hill, Margot Hamilton and Bucknell, Peter A. *The Evolution of Fashion*, Batsford (1967)

Holkeboer, Katherine, *Patterns for Theatrical Costume*, Prentice Hall (1987)

Moore, Langley, *Fashion through Fashion Plates*, Ward Lock (1971)

Selbio, Robert, *The Anatomy of Costume*, Mills and Boon (1977)

Tozer, Jane and Levitt, Sarah, *Fabric of Society*, Laura Ashley (1983)

Wilcox, R. Turner, *A Dictionary of Costume*, Batsford (1970)

SOURCES OF INFORMATION

UNITED KINGDOM

The Lace Guild
The Hollies
53 Audnam
Stourbridge
West Midlands DY8 4AE

The Lacemakers' Circle
49 Wardwick
Derby DE1 1HY

The Lace Society
Linwood
Stratford Road
Oversley
Alcester
War BY9 6PG

The British College of Lace
21 Hillmorton Road
Rugby
War CV22 5DF

Ring of Tatters
Miss B Netherwood
269 Oregon Way
Chaddesden
Derby DE2 6UR

United Kingdom Director of
International Old Lacers
S. Hurst
4 Dollis Road
London N3 1RG

USA

International Old Lacers
124 West Irvington Place
Denver
CO 80223-1539

Lace & Crafts magazine
3201 East Lakeshore Drive
Tallahassee
FL 32312-2034

OIDFA

(International Bobbin
and Needle Lace Organization)
Kathy Kauffmann
1301 Greenwood
Wilmette
IL 60091

EQUIPMENT SUPPLIERS

England

BEDFORDSHIRE

A. Sells
49 Pedley Lane
Clifton
Shefford SG17 5QT

BERKSHIRE

Chrisken Bobbins
26 Cedar Drive
Kingsclere RG15 8TD

BUCKINGHAMSHIRE

J.S. Sear
Lacecraft Supplies
8 Hillview
Sherington MK16 9NJ

Winslow Bobbins
70 Magpie Way
Winslow MK18 3PZ

SMP
4 Garners Close
Chalfont St Peter SL9 0HB

CAMBRIDGESHIRE

Josie and Jeff Harrison
Walnut Cottage
Winwick
Huntingdon PE17 5PP

Heffers Graphic Shop (*matt
coloured transparent adhesive
film*)
26 King Street
Cambridge CB1 1LN

Spangles
Carole Morris
Cashburn Lane
Burwell CB5 0EB

CHESHIRE

Lynn Turner
Church Meadow Crafts
7 Woodford Road
Winsford

DERBYSHIRE

Georgina Dolls (*16–20 in. dolls*)
173 Allestree Lane
Allestree
Derby DE3 2PG

DEVON

Honiton Lace Shop
44 High Street
Honiton EX14 8PJ

DORSET

Frank Herring & Sons
27 High West Street
Dorchester DT1 1UP

T. Parker (*mail order, general and
bobbins, small fan frames*)
124 Corhampton Road
Boscombe East
Bournemouth BH6 5NZ

ESSEX

Needlework
Ann Bartleet
Bucklers Farm
Coggershall CO6 1SB

GLOUCESTERSHIRE

T. Brown (*bobbins*)
Temple Lane Cottage
Littledean
Cinderford

Chosen Crafts Centre
46 Winchcombe Street
Cheltenham GL52 2ND

HAMPSHIRE

Needlestyle
24–26 West Street
Alresford

Richard Viney (*bobbins*)
Unit 7
Port Royal Street
Southsea PO5 3UD

ISLE OF WIGHT

Busy Bobbins
Unit 7
Scarrots Lane
Newport PO30 1JD

KENT

The Handicraft Shop
47 Northgate
Canterbury CT1 1BE

Denis Hornsby
25 Manwood Avenue
Canterbury CT2 7AH

Francis Iles
73 High Street
Rochester ME1 1LX

LANCASHIRE

Malcolm J. Fielding (*bobbins*)
2 Northern Terrace
Moss Lane
Silverdale LA5 0ST

LINCOLNSHIRE

Ken and Pat Schultz
Whynacres
Shepeau Stow
Whaplode Drove
Spalding PE12 0TU

LONDON

Sunday dolls ($^1/_{12}$ *scale dolls*)
7 Park Drive
East Sheen SW14 8RB

MERSEYSIDE

Hayes & Finch
Head Office & Factory
Hanson Road
Aintree
Liverpool L9 9BP

MIDDLESEX

Redburn Crafts
Squires Garden Centre
Halliford Road
Upper Halliford
Shepperton TW17 8RU

NORFOLK

Stitches and Lace
Alby Craft Centre
Cromer Road
Alby
Norwich NR11 7QE

Jane's Pincushions
Taverham Craft Unit 4
Taverham Nursery Centre
Fir Covert Road
Taverham
Norwich NR8 6HT

George Walker
The Corner Shop
Rickinghall, Diss

NORTH HUMBERSIDE

Teazle Embroideries
35 Boothferry Road
Hull

NORTH YORKSHIRE

The Craft House
23 Bar Street
Scarborough

Stitchery
Finkle Street
Richmond

SOUTH YORKSHIRE

D.H. Shaw
47 Lamor Crescent
Thrushcroft
Rotherham S66 9QD

STAFFORDSHIRE

J. & J. Ford (*mail order and lace days only*)
October Hill
Upper Way
Upper Longdon
Rugeley WS15 1QB

SUFFOLK

A.R. Archer (*bobbins*)
The Poplars
Shetland
near Stowmarket IP14 3DE

Mary Collins (*linen by the metre, and made up articles of church linen*)
Church Furnishings
St Andrews Hall
Humber Doucy Lane
Ipswich IP4 3BP

E. & J. Piper (*silk, embroidery and lace thread*)
Silverlea
Flax Lane
Glemsford CO10 7RS

SURREY

Needle and Thread
80 High Street
Horsell
Woking GU21 4SZ

Needlestyle
5 The Woolmead
Farnham GU9 7TX

SUSSEX

Southern Handicrafts
20 Kensington Gardens
Brighton BN1 4AC

WARWICKSHIRE

Christine & David Springett
21 Hillmorton Road
Rugby CV22 5DF

WEST MIDLANDS

Framecraft
83 Hampstead Road
Handsworth Wood
Birmingham B2 1JA

The Needlewoman
21 Needles Alley
off New Street
Birmingham B2 5AE

Stitches
Dovehouse Shopping Parade
Warwick Road
Olton, Solihull

WEST YORKSHIRE

The Doll's House Draper
(*dolls' haberdashery*)
PO Box 128
Lightcliffe
Halifax HX3 8RN

Jo Firth
Lace Marketing & Needlecraft Supplies
58 Kent Crescent
Lowtown
Pudsey LS28 9EB

Just Lace
Lacemaker Supplies
14 Ashwood Gardens
Gildersome
Leeds LS27 7AS

Readicut (*parasols, dolls, fansticks and dolls' accessories*)
Terry Mills
Ossett
West Yorkshire

Sebalace
Waterloo Mills
Howden Road
Silsden BD20 0HA

George White Lacemaking Supplies
40 Heath Drive
Boston Spa LS23 6PB

WILTSHIRE

Doreen Campbell (*frames and mounts*)
Highcliff
Bremilham Road
Malmesbury SN16 0DQ

Scotland

Christine Riley
53 Barclay Street
Stonehaven
Kincardineshire

Peter & Beverley Scarlett
Strupak
Hill Head
Cold Wells, Ellon
Grampian

Wales

Bryncraft Bobbins
B.J. Phillips
Pantglas
Cellan
Lampeter
Dyfed SA48 8JD

Hilkar Lace Suppliers
33 Mysydd Road
Landore
Swansea

Australia

Australian Lace magazine
P.O. Box 609
Manly
NSW 2095

Dentelles Lace Supplies
c/o Betty Franks
39 Lang Terrace
Northgate 4013
Brisbane
Queensland

The Lacemaker
724a Riversdale Road
Camberwell
Victoria 3124

Spindle and Loom
83 Longueville Road
Lane Cove
NSW 2066

Tulis Crafts
201 Avoca Street
Randwick
NSW 2031

New Zealand

Peter McLeavey
P.O. Box 69.007
Auckland 8

USA

Arbor House
22 Arbor Lane
Roslyn Heights
NY 11577

Baltazor Inc.
3262 Severn Avenue
Metairie
LA 7002

Beggars' Lace
P.O. Box 481223
Denver
Colo 80248

Berga Ullman Inc.
P.O. Box 918
North Adams
MA 01247

Happy Hands
3007 S.W. Marshall
Pendleton
Oreg 97180

International Old Lacers Inc.
124 West Irvington Place
Denver
Colo 80223-1539

The lacemaker
23732-G Bothell Hwy, SE
Bothell
WA 98021

Lace Place de Belgique
800 S. W. 17th Street
Boca Raton
FL 33432

Lacis
3163 Adeline Street
Berkeley
CA 94703

Robin's Bobbins
RT1 Box 1736
Mineral Bluff
GA 30559-9736

Robin and Russ
Handweavers
533 North Adams Street
McMinnville
Oreg 97128

The Unique And Art Lace
   Cleaners
5926 Delman Boulevard
St Louis
MO 63112

Unicorn Books
Glimakra Looms 'n Yarns Inc.
1304 Scott Street
Petaluma
CA 94954-1181

Van Sciver Bobbin Lace
130 Cascadilla Park
Ithaca
NY 14850

The World in Stitches
82 South Street
Milford
N.H. 03055

INDEX

beading 65
Bedfordshire, collar 57
    edges 25–7
    lappet 44
Brussels stitch 29
Brussels stitch, corded 29
Brussels stitch, double 29
Bucks point, basic 9
    circles 37–41
    collars 56, 59, 58–61
    edges 17–21
    fans 73–5
    insertions 13–15
    lappets 42–4
    parasol 84
    shawl 92–3
    sleeve borders 45–8

Carrickmacross, basic 33
    bonnet 41
    collar 63
    edges 33
    fan 77
    looped edge 88
    parasol 87–8
cavalier pattern 110–11
chemise 106
corset 105

edgings, Carrickmacross 33
    Limerick 35
    needle 30
    others 17–27
    simple 10–12

fan mounting 79
flower technique 13, 21

insertions 13–16

lappets 42–4
Limerick, edges 36
    fillings 96
    veil 95

mittens 47–8

needlelace, bars 28
    basic 28
    collars 64, 67, 68
    edges 30
    fans 77, 79
    parasol 89

stitches 29, 65, 76, 78
wheels 65

pantaloons 107
parasol lining 90
pea stitch 76
pelerine collar 60, 114
plastron 53

Regency, dress 7, 34, 35
    pattern 112–13
    sleeve 49
    ruffles 49–51

Stuart, dress 31
    pattern 108–9

Torchon, edge 24
    fans 69–73
    parasol 81–5

Victorian, early 114–15
    mid 116–18
    late 119–20